An Inside Job

Revelations of a Supply Teacher

Grant J. Kersey

Copyright © Grant J. Kersey 2023

All Rights Reserved.

Grant J. Kersey has asserted his right to be identified as the author of this Work in accordance with the Copyright, Designs and Patents Act 1988.

This book is a memoir. The events recorded and described in this book are real life stories based upon the author's present recollections of personal experiences, observations and conversations with numerous colleagues in education. This includes conversations regarding matters of education with his wife, who has been teaching at various primary school settings for over thirty years. This book also includes personal experiences from his youth and when he served as a police officer. Again, they are based upon his present recollections.

Some experiences and opinions shared also include quotes from renowned individuals, who have been duly credited in the book.

For safeguarding and General Data Protection Regulations, all children's names have been changed or omitted. The one exception is where the author has written consent from a parent to include a letter to the author from her child.

For the same reasons, the author has only included the names of former colleagues, both in education and in law enforcement, where he has their written consent. For all other former colleagues, the names have either been changed or no name is used.

Furthermore, the names of schools where he has completed any assignments as a supply teacher, have all been omitted, as requested by the supply agency that he was employed by during this period. In addition, the name of that supply agency, it's owners and his line manager, have also been omitted, again according to the wishes of those owners.

As an added note, some schools name their Teaching Assistants, as Adult Support Workers or Learning Support Assistants. For the sake of fluency, the author has referred to all of these as Teaching Assistants (TAs), unless they are a Higher Learning Teaching Assistant, in which case they are referred to as a HLTA.

Dedicated to all the hardworking and selfless teachers in the Education System

Table of Contetnts

Preface	*6*
Lesson 1 – **Kindness** *What A Wonderful World*	*14*
Lesson 2 – **Humour** *Make 'Em Laugh*	*60*
Lesson 3 – **Awareness** *What's Going On?*	*79*
Lesson 4 – **Vulnerability** *Help!*	*100*
Lesson 5 – **Trust** *Don't Stop Believin'*	*139*
Lesson 6 – **Positivity** *Don't Worry, Be Happy*	*174*
Lesson 7 – **Teamwork** *We Are The Champions*	*200*
Epilogue	*230*
References	*236*
Acknowledgements	*237*
Song Titles & Permissions	*238*
About the Author	*239*

Preface

Early one spring morning in 2015, as I entered a Year Three classroom, Lana, the class teacher, was busy getting things ready for the day. As she hastily moved around, I could see that she was visibly distressed, and I could tell she had been crying. Pain was etched on her face. Calling her by name, I asked if she was okay. At first, she replied that she was fine. Moments later, I asked if there was anything I could do to help. Lana then paused and came closer to me. In a soft voice, she explained that in addition to her everyday workload, she had just been told to organise a class assembly which was to be performed in front of the whole school in three weeks' time. Heavily pregnant too, she felt completely at a loss. Standing there in front of her and looking into her eyes, I felt complete empathy for her and the predicament she was in. I knew that words of comfort would not really be adequate or remove her sense of feeling overwhelmed, so without hesitation, I offered to take this specific challenge from her.

"I'll do it!" I exclaimed.

"But Grant, are you sure? There is so much to do and so little time." she responded.

"Yes, absolutely!" I assured her. "I will speak to Simon (the deputy head) and confirm with him that I am taking this on for you. You won't need to worry about a thing."

Taking responsibility for organising an assembly is not a job normally expected of a supply teacher, unless they are covering the class long term. I was covering Lana's class for just one day a week for that term until she went on maternity leave. Yet I knew she needed support. Lana's relief and gratitude was immediate and obvious. I had literally lifted a heavy burden from her shoulders. It was a small task for me, but a huge burden had been lifted for Lana.

These assemblies are fabulous opportunities for children to showcase their work, but the time it takes to write a script, find or make props and costumes, create backdrops and other resources, as well as fitting in rehearsals during the busy school timetable, can be incredibly demanding and highly stressful for the teacher.

I started work on the assembly script that very evening. As well as writing the script, I delegated assignments to the teaching assistant (TA), who helped organise the props and costumes. Ensuring availability on the hall timetable, I also supervised the weekly rehearsals each Friday.

The assembly included a speaking part for each child, some poetry from several children, a Bake-Off cupcake decorating game where their colourful, creatively decorated cupcakes, were displayed on a large interactive screen via a visualiser. The whole school, and the visiting parents, were then invited to vote for their favourite decorated cupcake. In addition, I located a video clip based upon the theme of the assembly - Red Nose Day, and created a PowerPoint presentation too. Lana was delighted with the final result, as were both the headteacher and deputy head. I was happy to have been able to help reduce Lana's workload.

Lana initially felt insurmountable pressure, and sadly, I have to say that her frustration and stressful reaction is not unusual among educators, particularly teachers, from my experience. The education system is at a breaking point, and too many teachers feel that as their workload increases from continuous extra demands, they feel less supported and less appreciated. Some don't even make it past the first year of teaching, even with support from the school.

The reasons are varied, but they can include long working hours, especially in the evenings and weekends, combined with the demands and expectations from other colleagues, leadership, government, outside agencies and even parents.

The constant moving of curriculum goalposts by successive governments has not helped either. It can feel like juggling with one arm, while more tasks and responsibilities are constantly tossed their way.

However, it is not just teachers who can feel swamped. Numerous TAs and senior leadership, including headteachers, are physically drained and mentally exhausted too. When there is unbearable stress, mental health and well-being is at great risk of declining, and the passion for the job often decreases. Their frustration and stress can easily be missed, but they are expected to just keep going and just keep giving.

Furthermore, schools are run on a tight budget, and I have seen so many schools struggle with resources and lack of personnel. The resources are often so low that many teachers resort to purchasing their own classroom resources out of their own pocket.

Consequently, a large number of teachers are seeking more flexible positions, and I do not exaggerate when I say that I have been approached by full-time and part-time teachers on countless occasions, to share my thoughts on supply teaching. I always keep such discussions confidential and never divulge private discussions with anyone else. As a result, many educators over the years have learnt to trust me and seek my views.

Despite these pressures, I have seen so much evidence of good practice in schools, and this book draws upon some of the positives and the negatives in the education system right now. I also discuss the impact that parents can have on educators' wellbeing, as well as their child's learning.

Another underlying thread in this book, is how I as a supply teacher, have assisted colleagues, and contributed to the learning and joy of the children entrusted to my care at school. Whether in school for a day, a week, or a whole term or more, cover teachers can foster a positive presence and make a significant difference. It is about putting myself in the 'shoes' of the teacher I am covering for, and being an exceptional supply teacher, rather than simply an average supply teacher.

For added interest, I also share several experiences from my years as a police officer in London's Metropolitan Police Service, and a few brief experiences from my youth. All these stories relate to the given subject I am discussing and are thoughtfully entwined within the educational stories and points of view I discuss.

So why would a qualified teacher with a 2:1 degree in Primary Education, choose to be a supply teacher after teaching full-time for only two years? Well, the reasons related to my personal health. My job consumed my life! Full-time teaching was so time and labour intensive, that there was no work/life balance for me. Almost every Friday after work, I would place 60-90 exercise books in a very large and strong bag in the boot of my car. I'd have the best intentions of marking the entire 'mountain' at home over the weekend but occasionally, due to other priorities or simply from just being too tired, the books would remain sat in the boot of my car going on a 'joyride' from one destination to another on Saturday and Sunday. On Monday morning, I would feel guilty that I hadn't taken several hours out of my busy weekend to mark the books, as I placed them back in the classroom. As a consequence, there'd be double the marking for that week!

The extra hours of schoolwork each weekday evening, took its toll on my physical and mental health, as well as on my family. As many educators will understand, it can be hard balancing life when both you and your partner are full-time teachers. Who minds the children, and helps them with their homework in the evening, when you both have pressing schoolwork to complete by the following day? Something needed to give!

The advice to "slow down" by a cardiologist, after being admitted to hospital for a few days, was an epochal moment for me. Several months later, after receiving that advice, I left full-time teaching and moved across to supply teaching. I believe I have a natural gift for working with children, and therefore didn't want to leave the profession entirely. I still had much to offer as a teacher.

After an initial application and two interviews with the owners of a local supply teacher recruitment agency, I was officially made a supply teacher on the 1st of September 2013. I was fortunate enough to join a fantastic supply recruitment agency.

I must admit that at first there was some apprehension, which was only natural. I worried whether I would be allocated enough work. I questioned my own abilities. Would I be good enough? Could I handle having to make quick mental notes of teachers' plans? Could I hit the ground running and confidently take over? Was my subject knowledge up to scratch? Would I be popular enough that schools would invite me back? All these questions, and more, raced through my mind. However, as will be shared later in the book, I had become accustomed to dealing with the unknown, and taking many 'leaps of faith' in my life. Therefore, I tried to remain optimistic despite my initial reservations.

I am now in my tenth year of supply teaching, and I have enjoyed teaching every year group, from Early Years to Year Six. On a few occasions, I have even been entrusted with teaching secondary school students. My line manager once told me that I am the agency's go-to when they needed to send someone who can best represent the high standards of the agency to a new school. I am in demand, and very grateful to be the first choice for many schools in the surrounding region. What's more, I love my job!

On seeing how positive I am at work, another supply teacher suggested that I write a book about my experiences. Coincidentally, this encouragement was echoed by my amazing line manager, shortly after in 2017. Their kind comments prompted me about a year later, to finally sit down and start formulating ideas to begin writing my very first book.

My real-life stories have been categorised into chapters relating to the qualities which I believe have helped me not only in my profession, but in some instances, an individual who has successfully overcome great adversity in life.

Perhaps this book is the long-awaited 'prophecy' made by Mr Thomas, an English teacher of mine in secondary school. He was an interesting character: skinny and short in stature, with a striking black beard and a tanned complexion. He had some unusual and eye-catching oddities, such as his habit of frequently picking his nose in front of us. We did find that eccentricity secretly amusing. Nevertheless, he was a friendly and pleasant teacher, highly skilled in his art, and an educator who instilled a love of writing in me at the time.

One evening, after a Parents' Evening, my dad approached me at home, and confidently said, "We met with your English teacher and guess what he told us?"

"What did he say?" I curiously replied, as I stood there doing the washing up.

"He told us that one day you would be a great writer because you have an amazing gift at writing, especially creative writing," he said proudly.

Mr Thomas, thank you for your faith in me! A great writer might be pushing it, but there is nothing wrong in daring to dream. Wherever you are now, I hope I do you proud with this, my first book.

Lesson 1

Kindness

What A Wonderful World

It was a typical shift for me, one night in 1994: mundane and nothing too exciting happening. I was alone and driving an unimpressive Austin Metro marked police car around the dimly lit streets of East London. There was not a soul around. All was quiet. Suddenly, the silence was interrupted by a call over my personal radio. Reports of an intruder at a local timber yard had been given to police. I was just around the corner from the yard, and the first to respond over the radio. "Yeah, 403 will take that. I am a minute away." Pulling up outside the locked gates, I turned down the volume on my radio and stood still for a brief moment. I was listening for any noise of a disturbance, such as the crunching of broken glass underfoot. Focusing my eyes beyond the gates, I could see a silhouette standing in a narrow doorway passage, reflected by the night security light at the premises. Squeezing between a gap in the gates, I quietly radioed that I could see a suspect. Within moments, I had apprehended the suspect alone. Despite his height and muscular build, Jason put up no resistance to me. He was a known burglar in his twenties, but this was the first time I had ever met him in person.

Other units soon arrived, and Jason was transported by van to one of the local police stations. Being the arresting officer, I accompanied him in the rear of the van. In those days, officers could sit in the van with the suspects. Now the vans have specially adapted individual cells for added security.

In the Custody Suite, Jason was processed, interviewed and all the usual checks and reports were carried out by me. A few hours later, he was bailed to return to the police station. As he was leaving the Custody Suite, Jason looked at the Custody Sergeant, Sgt Jolly, and declared, "You shouldn't be the sergeant, he should!" as he pointed at me. My sergeant, who was the most likeable sergeant on the entire Division, simply smiled and ignored the comment. I felt a little embarrassed by the remark and said nothing.

Why did Jason make such a statement? It certainly wasn't because Sgt Jolly had mistreated him in any way. Sgt Jolly had been respectful and professional towards Jason throughout his detention. Neither was it the way I had handled the situation at the timber yard, or how I carried out all the subsequent police procedures. I believe it was because of the way I had treated and spoken to him, and more specifically, how I had made him feel. Upon realising that he lived with a partner, and had a very young family, I had taken the opportunity to talk about his life, his aspirations, his journey, his purpose, and his needs. They had only been bite-sized opportunities because the priority had been to follow all the relevant safety procedures and protocol first. However, the several minutes in the rear of the van, a few minutes after his interview and briefly in his cell, had given me the chance to basically remind him of his responsibilities as an adult, and of his duty and care to his wife and young daughter. His young daughter would need him around. It was time to put the past behind him, grow up and get an honourable career. I made those pleas and gave other pieces of advice with genuine regard for him. I treated him like a human being, and he felt my sincere concern for him. I had touched his life for just a few hours that night. I gave him my time and I gave him hope for the future.

Every day, I meet people. Sometimes those liaisons are for fleeting moments, and I may never see them again. How I treat them and how I speak to them, however, may often have an impact on their day, week, or even the rest of their life. Love and kindness can go a long way, and I am convinced that being treated with these traits can have a direct impact on one's mental state, emotional wellbeing, and possibly even physical health. I have believed this for many years but was not aware of any medical evidence regarding the effects of kindness on our physical health, until a friend made me aware of Doctor Kelli Harding, MD, MPH, and her book, The Rabbit Effect: Live Longer, Happier, and Healthier with the Groundbreaking Science of Kindness, which provided evidence from a study by a post-doctoral researcher.

Quoting from her website, it says, "When Columbia University doctor Kelli Harding began her clinical practice, she never intended to explore the invisible factors behind our health. But then there were the rabbits. In 1978, a seemingly straightforward experiment designed to establish the relationship between high blood cholesterol and heart health in rabbits discovered that kindness—in the form of a particularly nurturing post-doc who petted and spoke to the lab rabbits as she fed them—made the difference between a heart attack and a healthy heart. As Dr. Kelli Harding reveals in this eye-opening book, the rabbits were just the beginning of a much larger story. Groundbreaking new research shows that love, friendship, community, life's purpose, and our environment can have a greater impact on our health than anything that happens in the doctor's office."[1] There is a feeling of inclusiveness, a sense of reassurance, and it seems, improved health benefits, from being the recipient of kindness.

As a supply teacher, the qualities of love and kindness are what I have tried to emanate in schools. A caring, helpful and friendly colleague helps ease the day along like a gentle punt along the River Cam on a warm, summer's day. If I'm not friendly and kind, then I can forget about being invited back to the school I've just visited. Whatever pressure I am under, I try to remain in control, and that friendly persona must remain with me throughout the day. Sometimes, that will be very challenging. If I've had a disagreement with one of my children that morning, then I leave that disagreement at home! If my bank account balance is so low that I have had to resort to peeling away spots of mould from slices of bread in order to make a sandwich, then so be it. If I have received

Lesson 1 - Kindness - What A Wonderful World

one of those unwelcome phone calls or text messages the day before, then I have to put that to the back of my mind. That bad day or week of mine can easily create a moody atmosphere within the class environment I am assigned to - if I allow it. Unpleasant moods, which can initiate unkindness, harsh words and spite, may sometimes leave a negative mark, even emotional scarring in some extreme cases. It befits every educator, including me, to pause and consider their words when under pressure, or when they are not in the best of spirits. Yes, sometimes I have needed to put on a 'painted smile' for the children and staff at school because that is what they need from me. Therefore, I enter school in an upbeat and positive mood, no matter what. Some days, it's an Oscar-worthy performance, but I find that even acting as if I'm happy on those challenging days, strangely yet quickly, lifts my own mood. As the headteacher of a school in Hampshire said to his wife, who is also a teacher, and whom I had the privilege of working with for a short period, "Mr Kersey! He's that jolly chap!"

Children respond positively to a pleasant voice, a smile, and an encouraging word or two. To praise a child would not just make their day but could have a far-reaching effect on them. In essence, my aim at each school is to assist colleagues with creating a better world for the children, by inspiring and motivating each child the best I can. Children need to feel enthused and excited about their learning and feel a certain amount of empowerment with their education. I am not saying that educators have to be best friends with every child, but we should certainly be friendly to every child.

Kindness and friendliness are effective ways for teachers to get children on their side. Children are then more likely to listen and respond to instructions when they feel their teacher cares.

While visiting a school, I saw an inspiring quote in one of the men's toilet cubicles of all places. The quote is from Haim G. Ginott, who was an Israeli schoolteacher, child psychologist and parent educator. He pioneered techniques for conversing with children. The quote is very profound, relating to the way a teacher treats a child, as well as the psychological and social consequences of that treatment, particularly if it is detrimental or negative. "I have come to the frightening conclusion that I am the decisive element. It is my personal approach that creates the climate. It is my daily mood that makes the weather. I possess tremendous power to make life miserable or joyous. I can be a tool of torture or an instrument of inspiration, I can humiliate or humour, hurt or heal. In all situations, it is my response that decides whether a crisis is escalated or de-escalated, and a person is humanized or de-humanized. If we treat people as they are, we make them worse. If we treat people as they ought to be, we help them become what they are capable of becoming."[2]

With some humour, I posted on Facebook in April 2019, how I had recently been described by one TA as having the,"…right voice for teaching." Then two weeks later, a TA in a Year Six setting, said my voice was, "…soothing and calm but authoritative." Then, on the day I posted the remarks, a TA told me at lunchtime, "There is something about your voice. You sound like a children's TV presenter." That made me chuckle! I wonder what TV presenter she meant – Roland Rat perhaps? Joking aside however, I found her remark and the previous comments very intriguing.

A calming voice has helped me countless times to quell an agitated individual. I remember the most powerful 'weapon' at my disposal as a police officer on the mean streets of London, was my tongue. I learnt to control potentially contentious, volatile and violent situations from escalating further, by the level and tone of my voice and the words I used. Sarcastic, offensive, ridiculing, condemning and abusive language, will likely antagonise some individuals further, and as a supply teacher, I try to remember this when faced with rude colleagues, parents and children. The right words and tone of voice can prevent battles.

Why do some children trust one adult in authority but not another adult in the same position? Well, the reasons will depend upon a number of factors, including their needs, prior experiences, background, and home environment. If their home life is emotionally chaotic and in disarray, there may be only a few adults who have an effective and positive influence in their life. All educators know that what works for one child may not necessarily work for another, but what is a common thread is that children need to know I am interested in them and as already stated – I care!

Lesson 1 - Kindness - What A Wonderful World

In the summer of 2018, I was out shopping at a local retail park, browsing the latest clothes sections at TK Maxx. While there, I met a former teaching colleague named Sonia. I had worked with her several years previously when I was a full-time teacher at an infant school. She had been assigned to work with a young boy, who was in care, and needed specific support with his day-to-day learning. His name was Brad. He was six years old when I first started to teach him and he was a complex boy, who exhibited attachment needs, craved attention, and had a strong sense of justice. For example, he would become increasingly and visibly annoyed, if another child, or even an adult, did not comply with a class rule or routine correctly. It was not unusual for Brad to become frustrated and have outbursts. He certainly had difficulty self-regulating his emotions and controlling his temper.

Sonia worked part-time with Brad, and would need to remove Brad from the classroom, during such outbursts, to allow him time and space to settle down, and also to enable the rest of the class to carry on and concentrate on their learning.

While chatting with Sonia at TK Maxx, she commented, "I always remember one thing you used to do, which was so nice and which I have never seen any other teacher do." Obviously, I was intrigued! With some curiosity, I asked her what it was. She replied, "Whenever I would take Brad out of class because of his disruptive behaviour and then return him to class once he had calmed down, you would always say to him, 'Welcome back Brad!' I always thought how kind that was of you and have never forgotten it."

That positive attitude of genuinely welcoming a child back to class, whether they have been removed for a short period of time, or excluded for a day or two, has always been implemented in my classrooms. No matter what a child has done earlier, the day before, or the previous week, it is vital that they feel welcomed back. It is important that they feel redeemed. If not, they may crash. A return to class should be a new slate and thus a fresh start. Where there may need to be consequences for a child's behaviour, will depend on the child and the school's behaviour for learning policy, as well as the circumstances and misdemeanour. Nonetheless, children need to know that there are adults at school who believe in them. When a child has been removed from the classroom in order for them to calm down and reflect upon their behaviour, I always try to make them feel welcomed when they return to class. Be forgiving to that child! They need to feel a sense of worth.

In June 2019, I was invited by the boys and girls from a Year Four class at a school in Christchurch, to join their football team against a Year Five mixed team. The game was set up during Golden Time, with a teacher on each team. At some point, I was asked to be the goalkeeper. With about ten seconds left in the game (the other teacher was counting down) a Year Five boy dribbled the ball past two Year Four boys and let a 'rocket' of a shot head towards our goal from about ten feet in front of me. I stood my ground and the ball hit me square in the face. A goal was averted, as I rubbed my slightly red face. The game was over!

Lesson 1 - Kindness - What A Wonderful World

The Year Four team rallied around me, as though they'd won the World Cup.

"Mr Kersey'" shouted one boy. "You are the best teacher in the world."

So, there you have it. If you want to receive the accolade of being the best teacher in the world, you need to take a ball to the face.

Nevertheless, any educator can still struggle with a particular child who they have worked hard with to 'get on their side' simply because some children may just not want to listen. Quite often I have had to deal with a child who can't keep their hands or feet to themselves. They distract others and disrupt the learning in class. There is no one solution, but experience has taught me how to deal with any given situation, as well as how to help each child use coping strategies specific to them. Let's set the scene. A child is constantly tapping their pencil on the table while I am standing at the front teaching the whole class. Perhaps I feel a little agitated. Do I ignore them? Do I rebuke them? Do I raise my voice at them? Perhaps any of these actions could stop the tapping occurring. For me though, I like to do the following, and it is very effective. While still talking to the class, I employ a subtle technique of walking up to the child, and gently taking the pencil from their hand. As I remove it from their possession, I position the pencil further away from them, and express my gratitude by saying, "Thank you for not playing with it." What I am actually saying is, thank you for letting me take the pencil off you. Now please do not play with it again.

It is positive reinforcement. If the child is tempted to pick up the pencil again, in order to play with it rather than write or draw with it, I repeat the action. On the odd occasion when the child refuses to hand it over, I stay there and ask for the pencil in a calm voice, with my hand held out. There has been only one occasion when a child refused to hand over the pencil. I chose not to create a drama out of the impasse situation there and then. Instead, I calmly spoke to the child afterwards, while other children were not around. We came to an agreement of how to avoid a difficulty happening again. The child appreciated a quiet one-to-one chat without feeling embarrassed in front of classmates.

I might say to a child, who has just flipped over a table in anger, after ensuring that other children are safe, "What's upsetting you, Nathan? Come and have a chat with Mr Kersey. Can we look at ways to prevent this happening again?" I have applied this composed approach many times, and it has nearly always been effective in calming the child and controlling the situation.

Why nearly always? Well, every so often, I will teach a class that has a child or more with extreme behaviour issues. How I cope and deal with those children will be a combination of personal experience, specific behaviour policy and practice, information from other adults, the tone of my voice, humour, gut instinct, discretion, and an equal measure of fairness and firmness. On the rare occasion when I have been faced with a difficult class or group of children behaving very badly, in order to gain control, I have had to resort to raising my voice. I have a booming, policeman type voice when it needs to be.

Lesson 1 - Kindness - What A Wonderful World

It's a horrible feeling when I have had to shout at a class. Such a reaction, albeit very rare for me, is not pleasant but was probably necessary at the time. Afterwards, I always consider what the trigger point was and reflect upon the build up to the outburst. Perhaps an outsider would agree and consider my reaction as entirely appropriate. However, fellow educators understand that in such a situation we must assess whether we acted correctly. I always ensure afterwards that the child understands they are not bad, but that their behaviour greatly disappointed me. Occasionally, educators have to raise their voice in order to gain control of an unruly situation.

In all the hundreds of different classes and settings I have taught in my years of supplying, there were a few occasions when I unfortunately lost control. Not of myself, but of the class. The children's overall behaviour in the class, was so extreme, so shocking and so violent, that no matter what measures or behaviour control techniques I used to try to control them, they just would not listen. To this day, they are still the most behaviourally challenged classes I have ever taught, and I have taught in schools based in London, Essex, Hampshire, Dorset and Yorkshire. As a result, I had to walk out of the classroom because of safeguarding reasons. I will share the experiences of those classes with you later in the book.

From time to time, but fortunately not very often, I have come across a colleague, who seems to constantly criticise a certain child. Perhaps they have become so frustrated and despondent with that child, that they are not fully aware of their almost constant barracking.

In the autumn of 2019, I was asked to work a morning within a Year 4 setting at a primary school in Poole. For some reason, one of the Higher Learning Teaching Assistants (HLTA) was teaching that morning, so I was just needed as classroom support. I had no problem with that. I have seen several HLTAs teach very good lessons.

I quickly observed a girl in the class, named Macy, who seemed to be on the periphery of her peers and the learning. When asked any question or instruction, she remained mute and frozen. I sensed she lacked self-esteem and was very anxious within the class. I noticed that for each given task, she was always hesitant to begin. I had compassion on her. However, what disappointed me greatly, was the reaction from the HLTA, who frequently criticised her and threatened her with consequences, such as her name being moved down the behaviour chart or staying in at break.

One of the tasks was for each child to write notes in their textbook, while watching a videoclip about volcanoes. A difficult task for some adults, let alone an eight-year-old, and needless to say, the girl struggled. There was a TA, who was not supporting any child, and just sitting on top of one of the tables, who was fully aware of Macy's dilemma, but who offered her no support. I decided to move over to Macy and, quietly sitting down on the floor next to her, offered her support. A gentle voice of encouragement was whispered, and a hand of reassurance was extended. I wrote a few sentences on my whiteboard, which she was able to slowly record in her textbook. Disappointingly, instead of praising Macy's best efforts, the HLTA chose to keep her in during play time anyway. I agree that the HLTA knew the girl better than I did. Yet, it was clear to me that the child needed help. There was no obvious support forthcoming for her from either adult, and it appeared that unintentional parameters for her had formed. Why didn't the TA, who was not supporting any child, come over and politely encourage her? Such children, if continuously frowned upon, criticised and condemned, may grow resentful of adults and angry towards authority. Our paradigm must always be to consider all children's full potential and not just the top performers in class. Some adults label those children that academically struggle as being lazy or misbehaving, but that is not always the case. For me, I try to 'see' the children who may not always get noticed by others.

Similarly, have you ever noticed how we are so good at praising children, but we often forget to thank and praise each other? Just as children need a new day or a fresh start, so do adults. We need to praise each other more, and that starts at the top.

I saw pleasing evidence of this at an outstanding school in Poole, while working there in the early spring of 2020. Every Friday morning, during whole school staff briefing, the names of colleagues, who had been placed in the Staff Appreciation Jar, were read out. What a great idea! I had never come across that activity before. How wonderful for staff to show a little gratitude for a fellow colleague vocally with these 'shout outs', and in front of the entire staff, even for just a small act of kindness. We adults seek kindness, approval and acceptance too.

Kindness is a universal language and a global necessity because we all crave acceptance and love. Whenever we, as a family, have visited other countries, my wife and children know that I just love to become familiar with the culture. I show respect to the locals, and I aim to be kind and generous to them. I am genuinely interested in learning about their lifestyles, traditions and, being a 'foodie' I love to sample plenty of the local cuisine too! I grew up in a multi-cultural community, and appreciated then, as I do now, the fascinating and educating contributions from all ethnic groups.

It therefore should come as no surprise that I love teaching children from different backgrounds. How boring it would be if we were all the same skin colour and had the same customs and viewpoints. I strongly believe that experiences with children and colleagues from other cultures, can make one more educated, kind, compassionate, and open minded. When cultural diversity exists within a class, it can make for a very interesting group. Meeting and working with children from different cultures and backgrounds allows me to explore the world through their eyes, and dive deep into their stories and experiences. Children's varied backgrounds, social upbringing, economic status, diversity, and cultural traditions can help all children, especially British, to see the world from another viewpoint and gain new perspectives in the lives of others. Of course, it is a two-way privilege, and children from ethnic backgrounds also have the opportunities to learn about British traditions, which is just as important. When different cultures successfully live together in peace, harmony and mutual respect, it is like a rich and vibrant tapestry, woven together to produce an incredible piece of artistry and design: beautiful and magnificent on the eye and soul!

I recently read an interesting report about libraries in Denmark which invite people to sit down and listen to someone else's story. It is a human library where you borrow people instead of books. These intimate discussions are one-to-one, and involve story tellers who have perhaps suffered trauma, hate or persecution, as a consequence of their ethnicity, social status, upbringing, disability, religion, political view, diversity or lifestyle. What a fresh and engaging way to learn about our world. Apparently, they are popping up all over the globe now. Sometimes we are stuck inside our own bubble for so long that we forget there are many who have a different story to ours and are wanting to be heard. Every voice still matters!

From my recollections, probably the most diverse school I have ever worked at was a school in Bournemouth. It was abundant in cultural diversity, and I had the good fortune to work there for five weeks towards the end of 2017. The children came from countries across the globe, such as Peru, Syria, Spain, Saudi Arabia and Poland. Several members of the class had only been in the United Kingdom for a short period of time, and I had great empathy for them, especially those who struggled with the English language. I found their experiences interesting, informative, and occasionally sad and shocking. Hearing of children's difficult circumstances and experiences can make one feel humbled and appreciative of the relative freedoms we have here in the UK.

My expectations are very high in class, and I required this diverse class to work hard every day. Simultaneously though, as is my style, I introduced an element of fun and silly humour. As a result, they grew in confidence and ability. This was evident in their learning, together with comments from other staff. Despite only working there as a supply teacher for a short period, I had made a positive impact on the children. On my last day, many of the children scribbled messages on the whiteboard, and I was also presented with a large card from the class.

After the children had gone home, and while I was finishing the last of the marking, one of the assistant headteachers entered the classroom to express his gratitude and to reiterate the school's desire to request me the next time they needed a supply teacher. I told him that the class had been, "…a joy to teach."

While teaching for two terms at a school in Hampshire in 2017, myself and the TA had the opportunity of welcoming a new member to our class. His name was Omar, and he was eight years old. Omar and his family, which comprised his mum, dad, an older brother and a younger sister, were all Syrian refugees. They had fled their war-torn country, seeking refuge, peace, safety, and a new life here in Britain. His arrival was a stark reminder to me of the awful realities that many people, especially children, face in some countries and regions around the world.

Omar was a well-mannered and friendly boy, who unsurprisingly, could not speak a word of English. I believe the school and the local authority made arrangements for him to receive some form of help at home with his learning of the English language, and while at school, this responsibility was left to me and my TA, Trisha, who worked part-time. Initially, we received very little guidance from the school. Nevertheless, Trisha and I pressed forward the best we could with teaching Omar the English language. Trisha was a marvellous asset to him and the class.

There were other challenges within the class, and the children needed special attention for a number of reasons. For example, one of the children, named Robin, had a physical disability in the muscles of his legs, which caused him to collapse to the floor regularly. He would arrive at school in a wheelchair, and then use a walking frame in school. It was his parents wish that he used a walking frame, rather than remain in his wheelchair, in order to help strengthen his legs. This walking frame would be positioned right next to Robin's work area but even getting out of his chair would cause him to sometimes collapse to the floor. Trisha or I would then rush over to help get him back to his feet. He really needed a one-to-one adult. In order to make his environment more comfortable, I changed the class seating arrangement so that he was closer to the front of the class and to my desk. I was then able to be near him when he fell. In addition, there were several children who had behaviour issues, including a few boys who were prone to almost daily acts of violence and other extreme disruptive behaviour. Two of those boys were seated at opposite ends of the classroom. If they were near each other, it was like a 'volcano' erupting. It was yet another extremely challenging class for me! However, I won't discuss further the details of all those other challenges because I want to focus on Omar.

Each day, I would not only need to differentiate the English lessons between the Year three and Year four children, as it was a mixed year class, but I would also need to decide upon simple resources and tasks for Omar. Trisha and I, and occasionally other children, would read to him daily. We also used flashcards, picture cards and would model simple sentences with him. Carpet time was also beneficial to him. During the carpet time learning moments, he could see more closely the reactions of his peers through body language and facial expressions. Again, this became a great tool to help Omar improve his English and integrate within the class. He was very much loved and accepted by everyone, even by the tough kids.

A second TA was assigned to my class around February half-term. Sarah worked full-time and was a godsend for Trisha and I and the entire class. Although she had been assigned as a one-to-one adult to a boy with behavioural issues and attachment disorders, she also worked with Omar when the situation allowed. Intervention for Omar, while he was at school, was also finally put in place during this time. Over time, with all the adults, children and resources aiding Omar, his grasp on the English language gradually grew stronger and stronger. His parents were humbly grateful for all our efforts to support their fine son.

However, despite his brilliant progress, there was one area where he remained almost subdued and reserved. It was football. Over a period of time, I had noticed that Omar would frequently stand on the marked sidelines of the playground, staring at the boys in his class playing football. I perceived that he desperately wanted to join in. Time and time again, if I was on break duty, I would try and encourage Omar to join in. Each time, he would shake his head and decline the offer. Yet I knew that he was keen to play football.

Then one day, about three or four months after he had joined the school, he once again stood on the sidelines watching the football match in front of him. I knew he was hungry to play football. So, I said to him, "Omar, would you like to play football?"

"No!" he quickly replied.

"Omar, I can help you if you would like to play."

Once again, he promptly replied, "No!"

Putting my hand on his shoulder, I looked at him and said gently, "Omar, I know you want to play football. The boys would love for you to join in. I can help you. Shall I ask the boys?"

Omar's eyes lit up with excitement. He had been too nervous and shy to ask himself. He needed a mediator to intervene and make his little dream possible. I then called one of the boys over. This boy, named Mark, was a dominant force in class and I knew Omar looked up to him. I asked Mark if Omar could join the game.

"Yes, of course! C'mon Omar!" he said, signalling for Omar to join them all.

From that moment onwards, as far as I was aware, Omar joined in every football match at breaktime. Feeling noticed, loved and accepted by the adults in school, as well as his peers, was just as important to Omar, as the strenuous task of grasping the English language.

Just over a year later, in August of 2018, I met his entire family by chance, while on a shopping trip in Bournemouth. It was wonderful to see them all. I greeted them and gave special praise and recognition to Omar, whose English was fluent and clear. I engaged with his dad in conversation, and he expressed his gratitude to me. Handing me a piece of paper with his phone number, he said, "You're always welcome in my home. Come for dinner some time." Although I never followed up on that kind gesture, I did regard it as a great honour.

For each of us, we may not always realise the glorious 'blossom' which springs up months or years later, as a result of our tiny seeds of effort, kindness and empathy – but we carefully and painstakingly plant and nourish those tender seeds anyway, so that the child, and others, can benefit in the future.

Children, and especially primary school aged children, seek attention and affection. They will draw, create or make gifts as a way of saying thank you. I never leave these gifts at school because I put myself in the child's shoes. How disheartening it would be for a child to return to class the next day and discover that I had left behind the drawing they had spent time creating, and had subsequently given to me as a present. Neither do I throw it in the recycling bin. What if the recycling bin is not emptied that evening and the child's work is found in the bin the following day, by that child or their friend? I place it next to the teacher's keyboard, which is where I also leave my written feedback. It then reminds me to take the child's gift home.

I fondly recall in September 2018, spending a day in an Early Years Class at a school in Bournemouth. I taught the younger children for one day a week, over several weeks. It was such a fun experience. At the end of my first day, a little girl in the class came up to me and said, "I have made this for you." She had spent time sticking various adhesive cartoon character labels to a plastic water bottle. This was her simple but kind gift to me. I praised her lovely creative work and thanked her. That gift subsequently took pride of place on my study desk at home for quite a long period of time.

This gift from an Early Years Child (aged 4-5 years) remained on my desk at home for several weeks.

I once read a thought-provoking quote on social media about kindness. The setting looked as though it was a school in the United States of America. The photo was of a young boy standing next to a display in school. On the display were these words by Bryan Skavnak.

"Some kids are smarter than you.
Some kids have cooler clothes than you.
Some kids are better at sports than you.
It doesn't matter.
You have your thing too.
Be the kid who can get along.
Be the kid who is generous.
Be the kid who is happy for other people.
Be the kid who does the right thing.
Be the nice kid."[3]

A beautiful statement indeed, and the message is clear! Yet, kindness is not just for kids. As a cover teacher, I look for moments to be kind and considerate to everyone, from the office person I first meet as I arrive, to the cleaner in my classroom at the end of the day. Opportunities to show kindness and reach out to others are everywhere. All we need to do is open our eyes and hearts to recognise them and then act. It could be that shy student teacher who is carrying out their work placement, or a tired teaching colleague inundated with tasks. Perhaps it is a child who has had little sleep the night before because they are a carer for an adult at home. I may not be fully versed with the details of their life, in order to decide whether I am going to be sympathetic and kind to that child, but I don't need to really.

Nevertheless, depending upon the setting and situation, I can sometimes be privy to confidential information about a child which pulls at my heart strings. During my first year as a supply teacher, I had the joy of working with a Year Five class for the spring and summer terms. The school was set in Boscombe, and had its share of challenges. Despite the challenges, the school had a co-acting style of staff who gelled perfectly. There were achievers, perfecters, contributors and harmonisers, and each staff member was conducive to the school values and ethos. It was a superb school!

I soon became aware of the many individual challenges faced by some children in the class. One boy, named Lenny, seemed to wear the same shirt to school, day in, day out. I observed that the cuffs and neckline of Lenny's shirt were always stained black, and the shirt front would often have food and other marks on it. I was informed of the challenges surrounding his background and personal needs. Despite his loud voice and frequent discourteous outbursts, I grew to admire him.

To show kindness to the class, and as a way of acknowledging their efforts and further encouraging good learning, I decided to implement a raffle ticket scheme to reward good behaviour, acts of kindness or sheer effort. Such reward schemes are common in schools, and it is usually the responsibility of the teacher to purchase the prizes, often out of their own pocket. So that's what I did. I bought a collection of inexpensive gifts to fill a decorated shoe box, which I presented to the children. Each Friday, the box would be shown to the class and two names would be drawn from the raffle ticket box. Despite receiving at least one raffle ticket every week, Lenny would constantly miss out on a gift. As time went by, he became more and more downcast, as other names would be drawn instead of his. Over a period of months, every child received a gift, except Lenny. That was the luck of the draw.

During the penultimate week of the summer term, I decided to 'fix' the result to make sure Lenny would win. I made a great show of swirling the raffle tickets around, knowing I had his ticket already in my hand. As I showed the winning ticket, he made his usual defeatist comment, "It won't be me. I never win anything." To his surprise, his name was read out. He was absolutely delighted and eagerly anticipated his gift. He came to the front and chose a mini–NFL American football foam ball. For the rest of that day and almost every day of the final week, he had that ball either on the desk or in his hands. At break time, he would play with his new toy. Such a little gift was very significant to Lenny, and he cherished it. I was happy for him. I received the personal satisfaction of knowing that a small act of kindness on my part had made a big impact on his day. As far as I was concerned, it was about developing and nurturing the whole child, and I felt pleased with my best efforts not to forget him.

Another account of kindness I would like to share, took place at a different school in Bournemouth, in the summer term of 2019. I met a boy, whose class I had taught for the day, named Jacob. He was an obliging boy but low in ability for his age-related learning levels. Consequently, he lacked belief in himself. With Jacob present, I spoke to his mum at the end of the day. I remarked on how hard he had worked that day and praised Jacob for trying his best. His mum then mentioned that he was trying to improve his reading at home, and that he loved the Wimpy Kid books. I asked if she was referring to the Diary of a Wimpy Kid book series, to which she replied it was. She commented that they were trying to save to buy more books in the series because this would help him significantly with his reading. On hearing this information, I was immediately struck with an idea. I invited them both into the classroom, opened my bag, and pulled out a hardback copy of the latest book in the Wimpy Kid book series. Handing it to Jacob, I told him that I had purchased the book in America only a few months earlier, and that it had not been read or used. It was pristine and new! "It's a gift from me to you Jacob. Enjoy reading it and next time I visit your school, please tell me all about the pages you have read." Jacob was so happy and thanked me profusely. As he left the classroom, he had a beaming smile as he clutched his new gift tightly to his chest. Naturally, I was delighted for him.

Of all the moments when I have gladly reached out with kindness to a child, the following account is my favourite. It was the impact I believe I made on the child and his family which is so memorable to me.

You may recall when England and Wales hosted the Rugby World Cup event in autumn 2015. One September evening during this rugby event, I decided to wear my England rugby t-shirt on an evening date with my wife, Gill. Our youngest daughter, who was eleven years old at the time, questioned me for wearing a rugby top when I was going on a date with her mum. She, quite understandably, felt I should have dressed up more smartly. I reminded my daughter that it was the Rugby World Cup, and I would stick to my choice. To this day, I'm content with that choice because of how events unfolded later that evening. We took our daughter with us that evening, rather than leave her at home alone.

Following our meal, my wife mentioned that she wanted to stop at Tesco and buy some Friday night treats; a regular habit of ours following a busy week. We chose some treats, and as we made our way up the escalators to view the clothing section, who should be standing in front of us, but the All Blacks rugby legend himself, Jonah Lomu. I walked up to this six-foot five giant of a man, extended my hand and looked him in the eye, saying, "Jonah Lomu, it's a pleasure to meet you. My name is Grant." A beast on the rugby field, he was a gentle giant in real life. He shook my hand and introduced us to his wife, Nadene, his mother-in-law and their two sons. My wife and I then spent nearly thirty minutes chatting with them all. They were, of course, here for the World Cup, and Jonah was busy conducting radio and TV interviews, charity events, school appearances and other business matters, as well as attending many of the games, either as a commentator or VIP spectator.

As Gill and I are both teachers, the Lomus were interested in our opinion on local schools. They were considering relocating to the UK for work reasons. Nadene and I exchanged contact numbers and kept in touch during their stay in the UK. We then said our goodbyes, only to discover that my daughter and the two boys had decided to play hide and seek in and around the clothes rails because they were so bored with hanging around for us adults to stop talking. That meeting was such a fantastic occasion for me. The photo below shows me standing proudly next to possibly the greatest rugby player of all time. Jonah Lomu was a true gentleman.

My proud moment meeting the All Blacks Rugby Legend, Jonah Lomu.

After meeting the Lomu family, I decided to purchase a rugby ball. It was not any ordinary brand of rugby ball but a state-of-the-art rugby ball: a Gilbert branded rugby ball. My intention was to meet the Lomus again and have Jonah sign it. Sadly, that did not transpire, so the rugby ball was consigned to life in a box in my garage, with the intention of playing with it on the beach or at the park, on some future occasion.

About sixteen months later, I began a tenure working long-term as a supply teacher at a school in Hampshire. I was teaching a mixed class of Year three and four children (7-9 year olds). In one of the other Year three/four classes was a boy named Greg. He was a Year Four boy, and very large in height with broad shoulders. His physical disposition was probably quite intimidating for his peers. One day, I casually observed him on the school field while he played tag rugby during breaktime. I noticed that he possessed great speed and athleticism for someone of his size, and that he was equally physically strong too. I had identified his potential for being a good rugby player.

Soon afterwards, I approached Greg and asked him if he liked to play rugby. Looking at the floor, he just shrugged his shoulders. He stayed there. He didn't move away. I sensed there was some interest from him. I told him I had seen him playing rugby and was impressed with his skills. I asked if I could speak to his mum after school. Greg looked up at me and without much visible enthusiasm, agreed to my request.

I met his mother and grandmother, with Greg present, after school that same day, and eagerly shared my thoughts and impressions. His mum was grateful for my interest in her son, and said she would think about my suggestions.

The months rolled on, and I would see Greg around the school from time to time. He was a quiet boy who always seemed moody and forlorn, and he would frequently have outbursts of anger in class and around the school. I would try and cheer him up and would call him my England prop. I would stop to briefly chat and ask him how he was doing but Greg rarely made the effort to engage in conversation with me. Nevertheless, I would always make eye contact with him and find something to praise him about. He needed positive reinforcement, and he deserved nothing less than respect and consideration from me.

Then in early July of that year, while supervising a mixed ad-hoc tag rugby game during break, Greg eagerly asked me if he could join in. I told him to be gentle with the other children, and then agreed. He took everyone on and again impressed me. Afterwards, I called him over as we were walking back into school. I asked if I could speak to his mum again. This time he agreed more enthusiastically.

Later that day, I spoke with Mum after school. She too seemed to respond with more zeal than before. She asked if there were any local youth rugby clubs, and I said I would make some enquiries that weekend.

The following Monday, after I had failed several times to contact a local youth rugby club by phone, Greg walked into my class, and with his head held high, declared, "Mr Kersey, you will be proud of me. I have joined a rugby club!" I literally leapt out of my seat and excitedly asked where and when. Greg told me that he had joined a club that weekend. I congratulated him, and later spoke to his mother to find out how this had happened. She told me that they had been in the park the day before and had seen some lads playing rugby under supervision. She approached one of the coaches to see if Greg could join in, and after observing his rugby skills, the coach keenly asked, "Where has your son been all this time? He's a team on his own!" I encouraged him to attend all the practices, listen to the adults and control his anger. If he got upset, which he regularly seemed to do so at school, it was vital that he still kept attending and not quit. I once again reminded him that he had the potential to be a very good rugby player.

On the final day of school that year, and after establishing a few days earlier with Greg that he didn't own a rugby ball, I presented him with that same Gilbert rugby ball I had purchased nearly two years earlier for Jonah Lomu's autograph. Greg was chuffed to bits. I simply signed the ball, "From Mr K." I took a photo of Greg holding the ball and showed this photo to the Special Educational Needs and Disabilities Coordinator (SENDco). She had been working with Greg, and thankfully said, "That's the biggest smile I've ever seen him give. Could you please send me a copy of that photo so when he gets angry in class, I can show him that happy face?" I did just that a few weeks later during the summer break.

That afternoon, school finished early for the end of the school year. The deputy head entered my classroom and shared the following with me. She said, "I've just been joining the parents and children outside for the afternoon picnic and saw Greg throwing the rugby ball you gave him, with his mum. I then overheard Greg's mum say to him, 'See Greg, there is someone at the school who loves you.' Well done Grant, that was so kind of you." That was indeed a marvellous red-letter day for me.

The rugby ball, which I'd intended to keep and treasure after having Jonah sign it, had gone instead to a boy who had very little. It went to a better home, and I'm sure, if Jonah knew, he would be equally pleased. Sadly, I was unable to find Greg's mum to get written permission from her to publish the photo of her son with his glowing smile. However, I am content with the thought that I made a difference to him and his family. The personal joy and gratification for me was immeasurable. Reaching out to others, especially those who can give very little, if anything, in return, is immensely pleasing - and yet that is what educators do every day!

Interestingly, and also on the final day at that school, as the children presented me with a huge handmade card with all their names written inside, one of the difficult boys, began to cry. "I don't know why I am crying!" he blurted out. He then gave me a hug. Yet, I know why he cried. You see, he and a few other hardened kids resented me when I first arrived at the school, and they had colluded together to make life difficult for me. That they certainly did! These boys admitted this to me on the penultimate week of my time at the school. Each one, feeling regret and remorse, apologised to me. During my tenure, they had all gradually developed an affection for me. Their hearts had been softened, and this was no more obvious that what I observed from the most resistant kid himself, who was now crying because I was leaving.

You see, all the courses, impressive qualifications, professional training and staff meetings will have little impact on my effectiveness in getting through to a very difficult child, unless I genuinely care about his or her wellbeing. That child must feel that I care. All the children in the school, and not just those in my class, deserve my genuine interest in their welfare and learning. We teach the importance of the Three Rs in education, but I believe that what I call the Three Cs: compassion, courage, and a change of heart – are of equal value to a child's development as well.

Towards the end of another long-term tenure of several

months at a school northeast of Poole, the TA, who I had been working with, was chatting with me in the playground one day. Her name was Sharna, and she shared her thoughts about my interactions at the school and the influence I had had. During our conversation she exclaimed, "Everyone in this school likes you."

"That's lovely to know Sharna. Why is that do you think?" I enquired.

"I think it's because you are genuine," came her reply.

What does the word 'genuine' really mean? The Oxford Dictionary of English defines it as, "Free from pretence, affectation, or hypocrisy." I try to avoid being sneaky, sycophantic or attention-seeking, which do not make for good relationships or communication, either in the classroom, or among colleagues around the school. Being sincere and open, on the other hand, helps to establish good relationships both with children and with colleagues. Of course, none of us can please everyone all of the time. That's just life!

While on an assignment at a school in Bournemouth in the summer of 2019, I became engaged in a conversation with an American educator named Mary. She had qualified as a teacher in the U.S. and had taught there before relocating to the UK, where she had been working as a teacher for about twenty years. However, she was now employed as a Special Education Intervention adult at various local schools. From her twenty years of working in primary and secondary school settings in the UK, there was one thing that disturbed her more than anything else. Mary then shared the following with me.

She quietly told me, so as not to be overheard by others, that there was a distinct lack of kindness and love from too many educators in this country. She continued to say that in the USA, teachers are generally much kinder and calmer. That gave me much food for thought. Why would that be the case? I believe Mary was genuine and sincere in her comments. She had a vast amount of experience of teaching in both countries. There seemed to be a sense of urgency and desperation in her voice, as though she wanted to change the unkindness and harsh behaviour she had witnessed from some educators, whom she had encountered here in the UK, but was completely powerless to do so.

I have no doubt that the constant pressures on teachers has a direct effect on how we may sometimes speak and mistreat others. I understand this. I've been there on a few occasions myself. I have been abrupt and said things I have regretted. Which educator hasn't? We are only human! We have feelings too. However, we are expected to be impeccable in our words and behaviour.

I'm pleased to say that it is my experience that the overwhelming majority of colleagues I have worked with, have been very helpful and supportive. Nevertheless, albeit not too often, I do encounter someone who is obstinate and malevolent towards me. In spite of the good I try to do, a very small percentage of fellow educators will choose not to like me - let's just get that straight! It becomes their problem, not mine!

Lesson 1 - Kindness - What A Wonderful World

One reason could simply be that I am a supply teacher, rather than a contracted or full-time teacher, and a few educators resent the fact that, in their eyes, supply teachers should be looked down upon. It is such a banal but rare attitude, yet it does exist!

An example of this came on the final day of term one year, at a large primary school. I had been invited to teach for the day at this highly respected school. I had taught at this school as a covering teacher on a number of occasions, and I had come to love this particular school. It was one of my favourites. One of the joys of supply teaching, is the opportunity to teach in different settings, even on the same day. On this particular day, I was asked to work in an Early Years Foundation Class (EYFS) for the morning.

As the deputy head of another school in Bournemouth, Mr Day, once said to me, "We request you and Sean Pogmore by name because you can both effectively work from Reception to Year Six." Sean, by the way, is an amazing supply teacher and also a successful part-time actor, who has appeared in a number of television shows, including the hugely popular Poldark series.

And so, with delight and my usual positive persona, I attended the school. I expected all the staff to be in a pleasant mood, albeit exhausted from a long year of teaching, and deserving of an imminent summer break.

Upon entering the classroom, I noticed the teacher, Miss Chumpton, was in conversation with a colleague. I politely stood at a distance and waited. Eventually, Miss Chumpton looked at me, and sternly said, "Yes?" I introduced myself, and without acknowledgement or comment, she looked away and continued her discussion with her colleague. I remained silent, waiting patiently. Moments later, without a welcome greeting from her, she informed me that the children would be having a PE lesson immediately after the register and advised me to see the PE teacher for instructions. "He'll be in his office!" she asserted.

I set off to try and find him. Needless to say, he wasn't in his office, and I spent valuable time trying to locate him around the large school. I did ask a few adults and the reply was always the same, "He should be in his office." Finally, I did find him - not in his office - and he politely asked me to ensure the children were taken to the hall as soon as possible after registration. Furthermore, he instructed me not to allow them to change into their PE kit because there would be a very limited amount of time in the hall, due to an impromptu assembly. He informed me that I would be assisting him during the PE lesson. I thanked him and quickly returned to the classroom.

Have you ever entered an environment where you felt a sharp sense of 'chill' in the air? I am not referring to the absence of heating in the room, or a sudden gust of cold air. I am talking about a sense of dislike, even hatred towards you. I felt very uncomfortable re-entering the classroom, and I knew something was not right. Despite my attempts to engage Miss Chumpton in polite conversation about the children and the morning procedure, she just was not interested in me or my questions. I was faced with a passive aggressive teacher, and such individuals can be very insen-

Lesson 1 - Kindness - What A Wonderful World

sitive, stubborn and arduous to work with. She was colder than an Eskimo's brass toilet seat!

Miss Chumpton soon left the classroom, and I assumed she was just too busy to answer my few questions. Shortly afterwards, the TA entered the classroom, and I was grateful to be able to speak with her about any needs of the children. She was very helpful and named some children who had specific needs that I probably should be aware of. During this brief but informative discussion, Miss Chumpton returned to classroom, and, upon realising what we were discussing, firmly snapped three times, "They're fine! They're fine! They're fine!" I said nothing and looked at the TA, who seemed a little embarrassed or even ashamed that she had dared talk to me. Nevertheless, I thanked the TA for her time and the information shared.

The TA departed the room, and I was once again left alone in the room with Miss Chumpton. I continued to sense that something was wrong, and so I allowed her the time to do whatever she needed to do. I asked if there was anything I could do to help, such as set any resources out, but I was totally ignored. She didn't even answer me! One question I really needed to ask, which is common for me to ask, is what the children's early morning routines are, prior to the registration. I had meant to ask the TA, but that conversation had been abruptly cut short by Miss Chumpton. This information is absolutely crucial for a supply teacher to know. Miss Chumpton's reply surprised me. "I don't know. I'm not normally here on a Friday morning." I found that an unusual response, as she was their class teacher, and taught them for the rest of the week. Surely, she had some idea of their morning routine? I thought to myself.

Shortly afterwards, she left the classroom and joined a group of colleagues in a shared learning area. It quickly became obvious to me that it was Miss Chumpton's birthday. They sang, Happy Birthday to her and presented gifts, including a bouquet of flowers. She seemed very happy and thrilled, and with her gifts and bouquet in her arms, she re-entered her classroom. I thought a little humour might warm her to me, so I made a facetious remark, "Well, you really didn't need to buy flowers for me." My comment went down like a lead balloon. "They're not for you!" she abruptly replied. Yes, I know that! I thought. I was tempted to make a sarcastic reply, but held my tongue, knowing that her rudeness would likely just escalate, and I sensed she was also the type of educator who would then put in an unsubstantiated complaint about me to colleagues and the leadership at the school.

As a supply teacher, it is so easy for one's reputation to be maligned by false accusations and misleading accounts by a colleague, particularly when they don't like you, and they themselves are very popular at the school. Not only that, but as any visitor to a school will know, it is often best just to keep your private thoughts to yourself. Making waves as a visitor or newbie is often frowned upon, so I just remained awkwardly silent - again!

The children began entering the classroom at about 8.40am. I knelt or crouched down and welcomed each child into class. I introduced myself and provided the odd compliment, such as how much I loved their colourful coat, or their cool hairstyle. I even shook hands with a few of the children – this was before Covid. This friendly approach seemed to put some of the little ones at ease, as they were being met by a strange face. Whilst personally greeting as many children as possible, I observed how they would each place their personal items away and sit at a specific place on the carpet, which is not unusual for children of that age. I continued chatting with them as I watched them sit down. Miss Chumpton had not given me the number of children in the class. However, I had the paper register in front of me and could estimate that most of the children had arrived. Knowing that the PE teacher wanted the children in the hall promptly, I said to the children that I would like to start the register. This was at 8.48am. Miss Chumpton, standing in the middle of the classroom with a handful of parents near her, quickly spun around and curtly told me to wait until the bell at 8.50 before reading the register. I was not aware of this routine until that moment. How helpful it would have been if Miss Chumpton had informed me earlier that the routine was to wait until the school bell rang at 8.50 before reading out the register. It would have saved a lot of embarrassment in front of the parents.

At 8.50, and after the sound of the internal school bell, I started the paper register. While reading out the names, a couple of children were absent. I placed a slight dot in the box and checked with Miss Chumpton if this was okay. "Just leave it blank, don't leave a dot. Look I'll do the register if you can't do it," she dis-

Lesson 1 - Kindness - What A Wonderful World

courteously demanded. How condescending, yet again! I stood my ground and politely replied, "No, it's okay. I'll do the register, as it will help me remember some of the children's names." I felt so awkward again. It was like a battle of wits in front of some of the parents, and it really didn't need to be. The dissonance was still palpable, but I thought to myself, what the hell is she playing at? Stupid mind games? As Miss Chumpton tried to manipulate the situation, I seriously felt the urge to speak my mind, but that was neither the place nor the time to do so. Soon afterwards, I saw her lambast a child, "Sit down and be quiet!" In a strange sort of way, I began to feel some sympathy for her.

I reflected upon this whole episode afterwards, and without raising this with her, thought how I had been treated like an unwanted bag of refuse. Yet, how easy it would have been for both of us, if she had just been helpful to begin with, and informed me of those early morning routines and procedures, which I had earlier asked about.

Despite the fact that this individual teacher would only engage in conversation, which I had instigated, and then either ignored me or deliberately kept it very short, I had remained calm, respectful and polite. I tried to be friendly, without being over familiar, just as I am expected to be when invited to a school.

I would have been quite justified in assuming that her ego was getting the better of her, and that she was just a self-absorbed individual. However, as I mentioned earlier, that would not necessarily be the best approach, and is not my style. For all I knew, Miss

Chumpton may have been very tired and stressed. Indeed, we all were, it being the very last day of the school year. Perhaps she had just waded through a mire of challenges that week and was weighed down with an excessive amount of work to complete. Perhaps there were issues in her private life which were overwhelming her. Whatever the reasons, I could not know or surmise them. Therefore, when placed in such an awkward situation, I try to avoid jumping to conclusions about someone's behaviour or attitude. Instead, I offer any assistance, speak in a calm and respectful tone, and do not retaliate, or worse, get embroiled in an argument. In other words, I don't always try to chase answers when untoward behaviour or mean comments are aimed at me. I just try to be kind – with the occasional addition of humour!

Disappointedly, I discovered several months later to my surprise, that Miss Chumpton did indeed have some kind of loathing towards supply teachers. She had treated another supply teacher with the same contempt as me.

I was visiting another school and met a fellow supply teacher, named June, whom I hadn't seen for a couple of years. As June and I were 'chewing the fat' and sharing personal school experiences, she told me of a teacher who had behaved exceptionally rudely to her. It soon became apparent, that this was Miss Chumpton, who had been so uncivil to me on that last day of term.

June then shared the following account with me. She had been working at the school, where I had met Miss Chumpton, and, after settling her class in the hall ready for whole school assembly,

June sat down on one of the chairs which had been placed out for the staff. As the headteacher was about to commence the assembly, Miss Chumpton came over to June, stood right in front of her, and with her hands on her hips, abruptly declared, "You are sitting in my seat!"

I was keen to know what June's reactions were, so I asked, "What did you do?"

"I apologised and told her I didn't realise it was her seat. I then stood up and offered the seat to her and she quickly sat down," she continued.

"What did you then do?" I asked.

"I was so embarrassed, and I just stood there, while all other teachers were sat down. Fortunately, a kind teacher stood up and said he would get me a chair, which he did. Thank goodness for him! I felt so embarrassed and humiliated. She was so horrible!"

It was then that I realised Miss Chumpton was disparaging and ill-mannered towards supply teachers. She certainly had an issue!

Knowing what I now know, if I were to meet her again, would I act any differently? Probably not. Despite being treated so unpleasantly, I would still try to treat her with kindness and respect, even if it is not reciprocated. Saying that, I might be tempted to have a quiet and respectful word with her about her disagreeable manner. Why should I change my social graces just because she has a dislike for supply teachers? The strongest people decide to be calm and gentle, rather than responding with contention or anger, even when under pressure or treated with disdain. They have learnt to control themselves and not be easily offended because of what they have been through. They have learnt to govern themselves, rather than allowing others to dictate their reactions when faced with adverse individuals.

When a student teacher, visitor or new member of staff arrives at a school, even as a supply teacher, I always try to foster a co-operative and helpful attitude towards such colleagues, in order to help them feel welcomed and settled. We have all been there. We have each felt a tinge of anxiety and worry that kicks in when we enter an unfamiliar environment. That is human nature. Isn't it such a great feeling however, when we discover work colleagues, who are so welcoming and warm towards us?

In October 2018, I had the privilege of doing just that for a fellow colleague, whom I had been asked to support. She was a new teacher to the profession, and my line manager at the agency had asked me to 'show her the ropes' while I was teaching a Year Two class at a school in Poole. Apparently, the new teacher was lacking a little classroom confidence, so I put her at ease and showed her lots of 'Kersey Kindness.' I shared the day's timetable, discussed the individual needs of several children and explained who I wanted her to support that day. In addition, I shared an assortment of ideas and tips which I hoped would boost her confidence as a teacher. What a privilege it was to help a fellow professional in this way. I did my best to put her mind at ease and praised her efforts. She was grateful to me, while I was thankful to her, for assisting me that day.

To show kindness and empathy towards others is one of the greatest acts we can show in our day-to-day dealings with others. Be careful of judging others, who perhaps are not up to our own apparent level of standard, knowledge or expertise. As the graceful actress and Hollywood icon, Audrey Hepburn eloquently put it, "Nothing is more important than empathy for another human being's suffering. Nothing. Not a career, not wealth, not intelligence, certainly not status. We have to feel for one another if we're going to survive with dignity."[4]

The older I get, and especially as a teacher, the more I realise that what adults and children really need when they have done wrong, is not an atmosphere of whispering and gossip, or silent treatment, base ingratitude, mockery, criticism or condemnation. What they, and we all need, is unconditional love, open-hearted kindness, genuine support and sincere forgiveness. I try to understand those I disagree with or who have upset me. It is amazing the difference I have seen with their attitude and the change in mine when I do so.

On the whole, each of us are hungry for love, approval and acceptance. We yearn for a sense of longing and security. I strive to look for opportunities and moments to engage with others and reach out to them without judgement. Notwithstanding this, you may be the finest teacher but may still struggle with an emotionally broken child or a disgruntled colleague. Don't blame yourself! Just try and continue to love them, respect them, and support them, regardless of their response to you. We create a better world when we try to understand another person's different viewpoint. Love, kindness, understanding and a little humour at times, are indeed the cure to many of life's troubles and hostilities.

Lesson 2

Humour

Make 'Em Laugh

"Like the refreshing, soothing dew, distilled from the heavens onto a barren and thirsty landscape, humour can replenish the soul. It can wipe away a tear and replace it with a smile. It can banish the gloomy shadows and replace it with a shimmering of laughter. It can console a downtrodden heart and replace it with hope. Even if each moment is passing, it can still bring a much welcome transformation."

- By Grant J. Kersey

April 2020

The inspiration to write the above description, came during one of the Covid-19 Lockdowns in 2020. The month of April was remarkably warm that year, and I took advantage of the fact that the beach was just a short stroll from where I lived at the time. Those solace, peaceful, short walks, with the sun warming my face, gave me opportunities to reflect upon the progress of this book. On one particular day, on the return walk home, I considered the importance of humour in class, purely for this chapter. As I did so, thoughts came flooding into my mind for my own definition of humour. As the words and phrases came to me, I would pause, record them on my smartphone, and continue my walk, only to stop a moment later with more phrases and description, which continuously flowed into my head. It is amazing the inspiration that can filter through when one is in a quiet place. Alone. Pondering. Self-reflecting. There can be a sense of reverence and enlightenment during such moments.

While visiting a school, I saw a statement on a classroom door. It grabbed my attention immediately! It read, "A day without laughter is a day wasted."[5] Below this statement was the name, Charlie Chaplin. Chaplin, without doubt, was a comedy and song-writing genius.

Almost everyone would agree that it is important in most day-to-day work environments to have a laugh at some point, and this is definitely applicable at school. Even a giggle or a wry smile at someone's silliness or joke helps to move the day along. I like to think of myself as one who has a great sense of humour. In a school setting though, the humour must be appropriate, and my humour tends to mock myself, rather than others. Where administered felicitously, humour is the best medicine and always a win-win with children. They just love a teacher with a good sense of humour. I have regularly received the accolade of being a very funny teacher from many, many children. Humour can put children at ease, and this is very handy when they are unexpectedly met by a new teacher in their classroom. Such humour from the teacher, can psychologically settle and reassure the children, and make them feel comfortable with me. I become more approachable to them. Sometimes it is just the little moments of golden opportunities, which bring joy and laughter to children. Let me share a few low-key, teacher 'humour nuggets' of mine.

Occasionally, when I receive a note from a parent, I silently read it to myself, and make mental notes of anything I need to be aware of, while the child may be stood next to me. I then thank the child for the note, before jokingly pretending to read out the letter aloud. It goes something like this, "Dear Mr Kersey, we are so thrilled to hear that our child is going to be taught by the World's Most Intelligent and Handsome Teacher in the whole wide Universe. Best regards..." Inevitably, the child will say something like, "That's not what my Mum wrote!" They will then see the funny side and laugh. It has never failed!

Depending upon the class, I love to invite the children to read the daily register. They read it sitting next to me while I update the register. That all seems fine, except when they read their own name out loud. I ask them firstly to pronounce their name in a serious voice, perhaps in a deeper tone as if I were calling out their name. Then secondly, they would be asked to respond in a silly voice, such as a high-pitched voice. They love it! This is especially effective for children who are a little shy. It is a subtle way of coaxing them out of their shell. The children love this silliness.

Every so often, I am the unofficial referee during a football match at breaktime. If a penalty has been awarded, it will normally be a self-appointed boy who decides that he is the best player to take the shot. He will place the ball on the ground and step back in anticipation. I ensure that I am positioned right next to the ball, and as he steps or trots forward to kick the ball, I blow a 'raspberry.' I then look around and pretend to be ashamed of whoever did that. It has never failed to create a laugh among players from both teams – even the penalty taker!

Quite often the classroom humour will come from the children. Even the very young children sometimes mix my name up and call me hilarious names, such as Mr Curly, Mr Cosy, Mr Curtsy, Mr Custard and just prior to Christmas 2018, I was called Mr Turkey. The overall winner though, was from a Year One boy… wait for it… drum roll…Mr Nerdy! I loved all the different names and joined in the classroom laughter at my expense.

In September 2018, I had the following conversation with a small group of children, who had gathered around my desk one morning.

Child 1: "I hope you come back next week. You're not like normal teachers. They are boring and you are funny."

Me: (smiling and laughing) "That's so nice to know. I hope to come back next week too."

Child 2: "I like it when you read to us 'cos you use actions."

Me: "That's because I love acting out the different characters."

Child 3: "I just like your ties!"

Well, I was very happy that they considered me a funny

teacher and at least one member of the class appreciated my taste in ties.

On another occasion, while teaching a mixed 5/6 class, I was rotating around the classroom, following my initial whole class teaching input. My intention was to check and assess the children's understanding of the learning of algebra. Perusing their work and complimenting and supporting where necessary, I discovered a girl named Esther, who was reading a Harry Potter book at her table. She had no maths work to show me and had not even written the date. I asked her why she was reading a book instead of doing her maths and asked if she needed any help. She responded, "No, I'm fine! I just get grumpy if I don't read for a while!" I smiled and really wanted to burst out laughing. That was a truly brilliant answer which I appreciated. However, after complimenting her on her love of reading, I reminded her that there was a time and place to read her favourite stories, and that right now, we had maths work. She understood, and after a little further encouragement, she put her book away and commenced her maths task.

One important factor I have tried to apply in my life, is not to be offended when I have become the 'butt of a joke' from another person: adult or child. Where possible, I have tried to use that prank or joke to my advantage, especially when the prank was deliberately intended to embarrass or ridicule me. This was no more so than what occurred in November 2016. I was celebrating my birthday with my family, and enjoying a meal out with them all, when suddenly my mobile phone rang. I could see it was my agency, so I answered the call. It was one of the owners, and he asked if I would be interested in teaching a Year Three class the following day. I was delighted to and thanked him for offering me the work. He then proceeded to explain that it was Arts Week at the school, and everyone had been dressing up as artists each day that week. I had become known for dressing up in costume on dress up days at schools, which included themed days, topic days, school trips and World Book Day, so the suggestion to dress up, therefore, didn't seem unusual to me. The owner made it clear what the style was. "They don't want any of this Italian artist crap. They want French artists!" he professed. I accepted the challenge to find a costume and join in the fun.

For the rest of that evening, while at the restaurant, my mind spun as I toiled with what I could wear that was remotely French. My wife and daughters suggested a few items, and I managed to gather enough pieces of clothing later that night to produce an outfit that resembled something like a stereotypical French artist.

The following day, I drove to school wearing the outfit with a touch of makeup for a moustache, which I had drawn on my face that morning. As I entered the school, I introduced myself to the office staff, but they remembered me from a previous visit anyway. I must have looked quite hilarious to them as I proudly stood there dressed as a French artist. I checked that it was Arts Week, which the office lady confirmed. I then asked whether other adults were dressing up, "No staff have dressed up" she replied. "How about children?" I worriedly asked. "Nope, not children either." I realised there and then that my boss had set me up. I had a choice. Show my dissatisfaction or go along with the practical joke. I chose the latter.

Walking down the corridor towards my classroom, I came across a couple of teachers and decided to speak in a French accent. I also had to explain why I was dressed the way I was. Fortunately, they saw the joke and laughed with me. Most importantly, when I greeted the children outside, with parents watching, I referred to myself as, "Monsieur Kersey, the World Famous French Artist," in a French accent of course. Despite the embarrassment that I felt, I kept the act and accent going for much of the day. The children loved it and the staff appreciated that I was game for a laugh. My boss later admitted to setting me up and laughingly apologised. He did however give me credit for being such a good sport.

Two years later, I returned to the same school, and while marking some books in the classroom at lunchtime, a Year Five boy, who had been in that Year Three class two years earlier, walked past the classroom door, stopped and took a step backwards. Staring at me, he enthusiastically declared, "You're that French guy who dressed up as a French artist." I laughed and smiled, then suggested that the French artist was in fact my cousin, Monsieur Kersey. He smiled. I then asked him, "Who do you think was better looking, my cousin or me?" Without hesitation he replied, "Definitely, your cousin!"

I had made an impact on him, the other children in class,

and many of the staff, including the headteacher, two years earlier, on that day in November 2016. They all seemed to appreciate my sense of humour. Despite the embarrassment for me, I continued in character purely for the children's enjoyment and learning. The antics of Monsieur Kersey that day, will be imprinted on their minds for many years to come. A memorable moment for sure. Excellent résultat Monsieur Kersey! - said in my best French accent.

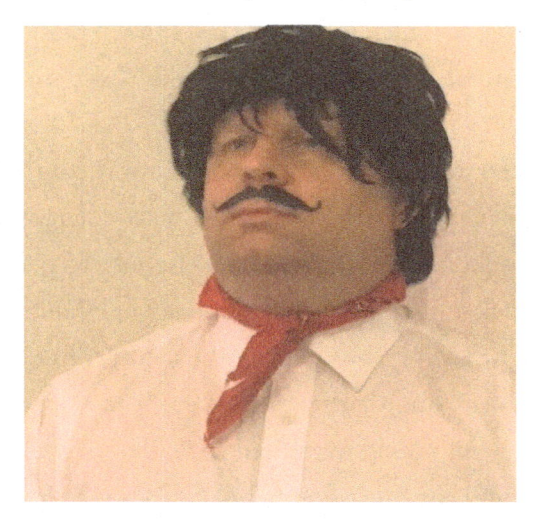

Monsieur Kersey: The 'World Famous French Artist.'

Any educator will empathise with me, when I say that I have been jokingly chastised by an adult in front of the children on a few occasions. While working at a school in mid-Dorset, in the spring of 2018, I had been chosen as the designated adult in charge for a day trip to a World War Two themed site. The venue was a mock-up of a typical World War Two village: school room, clothing washroom, grocery store, Anderson Shelters and underground passageways. I was responsible for about thirty children, together with six adults.

I had divided the class into three groups and, embarking from the coach, we made our way to the site, which was about a quarter of a mile away along a path. Upon our arrival, we were greeted by a bellowing air raid warden, who was actually a former army sergeant in real life, and now retired from the army. A woman stood near him, also dressed up in World War Two uniform and regalia.

The order was given for us to line up in our three groups, with the school adults at the rear. It was particularly cold that day, and, with a backpack on one shoulder, I chose to place one of my hands in a pocket. "And you can remove your hands out of your pockets straight away", shouted the warden. I, of course, assumed he was talking to one of the children as I looked around. "No! I'm talking to you, young man!" All the children looked around at me, together with one or two of the adults trying not to laugh. It was me! "Oh, sorry!" I commented with slight embarrassment. The children would remind me of that telling off for weeks and months later. One child, when asked at the end of the school academic year what her favourite moment of the year was, wrote down, "When Mr Kersey got told off by the warden."

Naturally, I did not wish to be chastised a second time by this former army sergeant, so after all the boys and men on the trip had been strongly instructed to always remove our caps and hats whenever we entered any room, I tried to keep this in the back of my mind as the day progressed. How awkward for me, but hilarious for the children, if I were to be corrected yet again. I did well to start with, but after a while my concentration began to slip. As we were being ushered into a room, where he was giving a briefing to the children, I was walking behind two boys, and had forgotten to remove my cap. The two boys had also forgotten this particular golden rule. Nothing got past this sergeant. "And what have you two boys forgotten to do?" yelled the sergeant. He was to their side and glaring straight at the boys. I was standing directly behind the sergeant, and whipping off my cap, affirmed what the sergeant had just said. "Yes boys. Listen to the sergeant. I can't believe you both forgot!" One of the boys looked at me and smiled. Then that boy said, "But you forgot as well Mr Kersey."

"Don't be so silly," I replied, in intentional earshot of the sergeant. "I would never be so stupid!" As soon as the sergeant had moved away from us, we all laughed together. They enjoyed that little moment of fun and banter, and I survived another possible rebuking from the sergeant.

While writing the manuscript for this book, I posted a message on Facebook to former school colleagues and parents of children I had taught. I don't make a habit of connecting with parents on social media, but I am connected to several whom I know very well. I was asking these people if they could remember any inspiring or funny teaching moments, or stories of trust, kindness and friendship to include in this book that they remembered from their working relationship with me at school, or where applicable, any experiences from their child while I was their teacher. One of the mums replied to my post by attaching a copy of a handwritten letter her daughter had written that evening. It was addressed to me. I was so touched that I thanked the daughter, via her mum, and sought permission from them both to publish her letter and name in my book. Her name is Amaelia-Mae, and she shared her memories of me when I taught her for six months in 2018, during a long-term cover at a school in mid-Dorset.

Amaelia-Mae's Mum posted this response on my post, "Please excuse her typos, she is pretty shattered and just handed me this. You must have been some teacher to her."

Lesson 2 - Humour - Make 'Em Laugh

Here is her handwritten letter:

> Mr. Kersey, one of the funniest teachers I've had in the 6 years of ▮▮▮▮▮ was probably the best teacher I have had. Some of the things that make him funny are his fun ways of teaching, his jokes that come up half-way in the lessons and his ability to keep up with the trend. But the real reason why I'm writing this is to explain exactly why he's funny, humourous and so up with the trend, here they are.
>
> Back in Year 5, + my class was doing maths with Mr. Kersey, our subject being angles and degrees. First, we started of with right-angles, obtuse angles and acute angles. After that he taught us about how right-angles were 90° and obtuse angles were -91°+ and acute angles were 89°-.

First page from Amaelia-Mae

Then, we played a game. Mr. Kersey shouted "90° to the right or 180° to the left or even 270° to the left. Though, further on in the lesson Mr. Kersey shouted, "360° to the right!" and because of the trend, everyone done a *360°. Mr Kersey got the joke, jumped up in the air and perfected a 360° degree turn. Everyone then started cheering and Mr Kersey bowed.

Another funny occasion, was when everyone wanted to see who could get the most teachers to dab. Coincidently, Mr. Kersey was out on duty. Some of year 5 stepped up to Mr. Kersey and all asked him to dab. Accepting it, he dab and everyone walked away, laughing and shouting

*It's where you jump in the air, spin, and do a 360° degree turn in mid-air.

Second page from Amaelia-Mae

Lesson 2 - Humour - Make 'Em Laugh

A couple of weeks later, we were learning about WW2, also know as "The War to end all wars". We dived in and out of topics to do with WW2 until Y5 got to go to Nothe Fort. We had to dre dess up as an evacuee. Back in the days, there wasn't any adult evacuees so he had to come as a boy. He looked hilarious and everyone laughed.

That's just about all I can recap in Y5 but I bet you are going to have even more funny moments over in America.

Yours Sincerely,
- Amaelia-Mae
Cruppy

Final page from Amaelia-Mae

Lesson 2 - Humour - Make 'Em Laugh

My humour is mostly intentional but occasionally it is unintentional. Like the time I was infamously given the title at school of the 'Vicar's Bike Thief.'

One day after school, in the spring of 2017, while teaching at a school in Hampshire, I was having an informal meeting with one of the members of staff, a friendly and dedicated team member, named Tom. While we were chatting in my classroom, two boys came to the back door of the classroom and banged on the glass panel. A little startled, I got up and opened the door.

"Are you okay boys?" I enquired.

"We've just seen a bike belonging to a girl in our class. It was stolen from the front of this school last weekend," came the response from one of the boys. Putting my 'Police hat' on so to speak, I questioned them further.

"What's the name of the girl and what makes you think it's her bike?" I asked. The two boys then gave me the name of the girl and explained that the colour, unique markings and model of the bike were exactly the same as her bike. I then asked where they had seen the bike, to which one of them replied, "It's down the road at the church."

With this information, all three of us, together with Tom, set off on foot to the local church, which was a minute or two away. Walking past the Tesco Express Store, where a few teenagers had gathered, we passed a middle-aged man who stared at us as we passed him.

Lesson 2 - Humour - Make 'Em Laugh

As we crossed the busy road opposite the church, I noticed a police car driving towards us. I waved and indicated to the police officer, who pulled over to the side of the road. "Officer," I said calmly, "My colleague and I are teachers from (name withheld) and these two boys are pupils from the school. They have told us that a bicycle over at the church, which was stolen from the school grounds last Sunday, belongs to a girl from their class. What is the best course of action?" The officer suggested we placed the bike in the boot of his car, and he would drop it off at the school. Almost immediately, he then changed his mind and said, "So long as those boys are sure it belongs to the girl, just wheel it round to the school instead." I then asked for the officer's name, just in case this backfired on me.

I collected the bike and said goodbye, both to the two boys, and also Tom, who decided to make his way home at that point. Wheeling the pink bicycle past Tesco Express, the same teenagers were outside, together with the same middle-aged man. This time, the middle-aged man looked at me with some curiosity, as I pushed a pink bicycle.

Arriving back at school, I searched for the girl's home number. After giving the description of the bike over the phone, the mum seemed excited that we had found it. Shortly after, the mum and daughter arrived. With a satisfied smile, I presented the bike as they walked towards my classroom. "That's not the bike!", the mum disappointedly informed me. Sue, the office receptionist, was standing several feet behind this mother and her daughter. As the mum indicated this information to me, Sue had a clear view of my face, saw it drop, and was in silent 'stitches' trying not to burst out laughing. In the meantime, I tried to keep a straight face, as it dawned on me that I had taken someone else's bike from the church grounds. Probably the vicar's pink bike!

I decided to return the bike straight away. Walking past the Tesco Express store yet again, with the same teenagers and that middle-aged man outside. The middle-aged man was now staring at me with suspicion, as though I was some oddball. I walked past them again trying not to make eye contact and feeling embarrassed to be pushing a pink bicycle in the opposite direction this time. I hurriedly replaced it where I had found it, sending a prayer heavenward that the vicar wouldn't come out and catch me. That would've taken some explanation! Everyone at school just loved that story. That's what I call going above and beyond the call of duty.

While on assignment at a school in Bournemouth, I had the most hilarious moment with a boy called Barkley. He often found it difficult to mix with his peers, due to his irascible responses and frequent, aggressive outbursts. While alone in the classroom during break time, he strolled into the room with a girl from his Year Three class. Barkley was often so highly-strung and volatile, that he had to be watched by an adult during breaktime. He had been given a daily task during break and had chosen a friend to be with him. The assigned adult was monitoring him from the corridor. I had taught Barkley in Year Two, and he had grown fond of me and my daft humour. He seemed to be drawn to me. As these two children entered my classroom, the following conversation took place.

Girl: "Mr Kersey, are you still the World's Most Smartest Teacher?"

Me: "Yes, of course I am! In fact, I have recently received another award."

Barkley: "For what?"

Me: "As the World's Most Handsome Teacher."

Girl: "Really?"

Me: "Oh yes! Don't be surprised."

Barkley: "But you can't be!"

Me: (pretending to look shocked) "Why not?"

Barkley: "Because of that."

Me: (showing some intrigue) "Because of what?"

Barkley: (pointing to my neck) "Because of the flabby neck."

Me: (pretending to be hurt) "I can't believe you said that about my neck Barkley."

With that, Barkley jumped back and let out a roar of laughter. As he did so, a piece of apple, which he had been munching on, came flying out of his mouth, and landed on my crisp, pristine, white shirt. It was the first day wearing this brand new shirt! Pretending to be shocked, I looked down in horror at the piece of mushy apple stuck to my shirt.

Me: "Uuuurrggghhhh!!!! What's that on my shirt?"

Barkley was almost crying with laughter, as I delicately tried to remove the 'mashed apple' from my shirt with a piece of tissue paper.

Barkley: (still roaring with laughter) "You are just so funny!"

As I walked out of the classroom, the adult said to me, "I haven't heard him laugh like that for a long time."

From then on, whenever I visited that school, Barkley would remind me of that hilarious moment, and would still laugh out loud as he reminisced over it.

In summing up this chapter, I found this quote from the author and philosopher, Emily Maroutian. It perfectly characterises humour, probably more eloquently than my attempt at the beginning of this chapter.

"Anyone who makes you laugh is contributing to your well-being. Laughter can shift you out of a bad mood, free you from worry, and put you in a state of joy, even if it's temporary. For a few precious moments, as your eyes fill with blissful tears, as you run out of breath, as your stomach muscles ache, you will have no other care in the world. If laughter is the best medicine, then funny friends are instrumental to our healing." [6]

As you have seen, humour holds a great deal of value in my everyday teaching. I have had tremendous success with building positive relationships with children, even challenging children, by being aware of when to aptly apply my appropriate comedy and satire.

Lesson 3

Awareness

What's Going On?

It goes without saying that being aware and informed of school policies, practice, acronyms and routines, is very important. Familiarity with daily routines and knowledge of how things work at school is vital for accomplishing a specific task independently, and for a smoother day. If the teacher has been organised enough to leave the laptop username and password (very uncommon not to) then it may be that I have to quickly decipher the route to access shared staff resources, programmes, or saved lesson resources on the teacher's laptop, if resources, such as PowerPoints, videos or worksheets have not been set up or printed. Sometimes, there is no laptop at all, yet the teacher notes ask me to share information and resources accessed from a laptop. That's when I resort to having to locate one around the school as soon as possible. Arriving early at school has its benefits!

Awareness could also be making myself acquainted with the class reward system, specific health and educational needs of some of the children or establishing what the school's marking policy is. Up to a few years ago, a large number of schools that I have worked at, were instructing their teaching staff to use two, three or at one school, four different coloured pens to mark the children's work. Two is fine, but when I have had to use three or four different coloured pens, I'd be sat there at the end of the day, focusing on what colour pen I needed in my hand, juggling one colour to the next as I read and checked the children's written tasks. As you might expect, I would sometimes end up highlighting a misspelt word in the wrong colour or writing a positive comment in the colour for negative. It was crazy! Many schools have implemented the practice of encouraging self and peer marking by the children, and this has become more and more common from my experience. Not only does this ease the workload burden on teachers but it is also empowering for the children. In addition, I have noticed a full circle in the last few years, where some schools have reverted to a marking policy of the teacher using just one colour - like it was decades ago!

Furthermore, awareness could be remembering all the start and end times for morning breaktime, lunch, and afternoon break, or what time individual children have to leave the classroom for their one-to-one music lesson or an intervention session. It could also be grasping how to use the school's printer and photocopying machine. Some machines need a degree to figure how to use them! I often make written notes of all these routines once they have been explained to me by the adult who greets me in class. As someone once said, "The bluntest pencil is better than the best memory."

Speedily adapting to these new routines saves a lot of time and hassle, both for me, the children, and my colleagues.

Being mindful of what time of the day I use the copier machine, and how many copies I print off all at once, is a sign of my consideration towards others. When the situation allows it, I like to print off the paper resources I need, on the day before the lesson(s). It is good to be organised! Nevertheless, it is inevitable that on some mornings there is an urgency to print off documents or worksheets no matter how organised one is. I recall on one occasion when I needed to print off thirty sheets for the children in my class. That was all fine, except in my haste I inadvertently pressed an extra zero on my laptop. Five minutes later, I went to collect my 'thirty' sheets from the printer, only to discover a queue of teachers frustratingly waiting. I commented, "Oh, there's a lot of teachers who need to use the printer!"

One adult replied, "Yes, someone from Year Six has decided to print off three hundred SATs sheets just before the children arrive." I quietly walked away pretending to be innocent, and stealthily returned to the copier machine, like some kind of secret agent trying not to be discovered, to collect the large bundle of papers when the coast was clear. My conscience got the better of me later though, and I confessed my embarrassing error, much to the amusement of my colleagues. Clearly, there had been no intention to cause any delay or inconvenience for my fellow teachers on my part, but nevertheless, my lack of focus on my laptop early that morning, led to this hilarious but awkward moment.

So much ambiguity can be caused when appropriate information is not provided by a member of staff. Collaboration and sharing good practice with colleagues is second nature with all good educators. I have frequently collaborated and shared good teaching ideas that I have seen working at other schools. I am amazed at some colleagues who act like 'Secret Squirrel' and hoard resources and great teaching ideas to themselves. What a skewed perception. It's not a competition. Let others shine too!

Fortunately, colleagues have mostly been brilliant at providing me with relevant information, as and when necessary. Occasionally, a specific practice may seem inconvenient, unreasonable or even unusual to me. Nevertheless, my philosophy is that whatever the school has put into place, it must be followed. The school wouldn't do so without good reason.

I remember a time, while teaching at a school in Boscombe in 2015, when a new procedure was introduced to the staff, that I personally found somewhat inconvenient. Any teacher, or TA, who would be teaching PE in the afternoon, was to arrive at school dressed in smart attire, then at lunchtime change into their PE kit so they were appropriately dressed to teach this subject. Prior to this decision, staff were permitted to dress in PE kit all day. Adhering to this new rule from the headteacher, was exactly what I did. It was inconvenient and time consuming having to go to my car at lunchtime to retrieve my sports bag, then head to the men's shower/locker room, and change out of my smart clothes and shoes, then put on my PE clothes and trainers. Then I would return my smart clothes to my car. Phew! This would take around 10-15 minutes of my valuable time during lunch, which was generally spent, as is the case for almost all educators, marking the morning work, tidying up, speaking to colleagues, and gathering resources and checking planning for the afternoon's learning.

After several weeks, I observed that a few staff were beginning to ignore this new rule. One or two even encouraged me to do the same. I felt otherwise! I represented my agency and was a guest at the school. To me, it was very important that I followed the rules and procedures, even if they seemed frustrating or inconvenient. I continued to change at lunchtime if I was teaching PE in the afternoon. It's not about what Mr Kersey wants. It is about what the school wishes.

Yet, there have been a few moments when I have been left adrift and was not made aware of a particular school practice or routine. Anyone who has worked at any educational setting for the first time, even if it is only for one day, will be required to read and sign the Safeguarding and Data Protection Policies. In my seven years of supply teaching on the south coast, I have worked in about seventy schools, and each school has had slightly different routines and practices. Not being familiar with general school routines and practices, has left me open to criticism on a few occasions. Let me share one example.

In the spring of 2015, I was asked to work at one of those

quaint, little schools, set in an idyllic English picture postcard village. A small, rustic church, an inviting country pub and a scattering of thatched roofed homes were all neatly laid out across the village. The location was very pretty. I had visited the school a few times over a period of about a year and a half, and always sensed that the headteacher was aloof and stand-offish towards me. I could not work out her reasons or fathom her mentality.

On this particular day, I was tasked with teaching a Year Three class. They were typical of any Year Three class, often excitable, keen to please, fun to teach, largely independent and a little mischievous at times. The teacher had left some handwritten notes for me, including the outline of the day. There was no adult support, which was not a problem for me, as I can comfortably teach without an extra adult supporting in class. The class next door was absent, perhaps on a trip, and since it was such a small school, the other two classes were located in portacabins outside.

The day progressed smoothly until we reached the mid-afternoon mark. I noticed from the handwritten schedule that the teacher had forgotten to record what time the school day ended. I had not taught at the school for several months, and racked my brain trying to remember the finish time. Remaining unsure, I asked several children who I felt I could trust. They collectively enlightened me with a 3:15 response. Fine! I thought. Plenty of time to get ourselves ready.

I like to be punctual, so at 3.14pm exactly, we headed for the exit where the children would be collected. This entailed walking along a short corridor, past the reception office and to the main doors. Suddenly, as I turned a corner, I was met by the headteacher. Bluntly, she questioned, "Why are you allowing the children out early?" I was a little shocked and apologised.

"What time are they meant to be leaving?" I inquired.

"3.20!" was her prompt reply.

"Oh, I'm sorry, I was told 3.15!" I responded.

Turning the children around, we headed back to class. Five minutes later, we were ready. Take two! We walked along the corridor, past the reception office and headed to the main doors. This time, there was another class in front of me. Great! I wasn't the only class this time, so I knew I was on time for sure. As it was a Friday, I decided to carry out my usual Friday custom, which I often did at the time. I would give each child a 'high five Friday' and then wish them a wonderful and safe weekend. I had only 'high fived' a few children, when, in front of the parents, the headteacher, this time even louder than before, shouted, "And we don't do that American stuff here!" What a myopic view she seemed to have of America. I was left speechless. Why the carping and haughtiness? Google and Microsoft were created in America. Was the school going to ban the use of these tech resources now? How ridiculous! I didn't say those thoughts out loud, but I was certainly thinking them. Feeling even more embarrassed, and in front of the parents watching, I quietly allowed the children out, while the headteacher kept her beady eyes on me, like a hawk waiting to pounce on the slightest error from it's prey.

After marking all the work for that day, and leaving written feedback for the teacher, I headed out of the classroom, with coat and bag in hand. As I approached the reception office, I saw the headteacher standing with a colleague. I stopped and gave my apologies for the 'high fives' and for leaving the classroom five minutes earlier than I should have. I didn't bother to explain that no finish time had been recorded on the teacher's notes for me because I suspected she would have just switched off upon hearing my excuses. I expected a gracious response to my apology, but instead she looked at me with some cynicism and replied, "Erm, okay!" Her face was about as happy as someone who had just swallowed a cactus!

I wished her a lovely weekend and quietly left the building. That disparaging mistreatment was wholly uncalled for and inappropriate. I honestly felt her behaviour and attitude was incredibly asinine, and it left me puzzled. Not everyone in a position of leadership and power is sensible and thoughtful! Despite my best efforts, there is no pleasing some people who may have unfair, or even ill-judged, preconceived ideas about me.

That experience reminded me of two important points. Firstly, this was an anomaly because the vast majority of headteachers and deputy heads have always been very polite, welcoming and appreciative of my work and contributions. If a member of leadership has a hang up with me, then that is their issue, not mine. I am always happy to discuss any concerns with any colleague, as long as they make me aware that they have a problem with me. I'm not Mystic Meg!

Secondly, I was also reminded, granted that it was the hard way, that one cannot rely on the children to be totally honest in sharing correct information. This can be yet another challenge for supply teachers: children taking the opportunity, if presented to them, to misbehave, mislead or deceive the supply teacher, where possible. To the children it is just a game. However, in the example shared, I should have been a step or two ahead of them. Ever since that moment, I have learnt the importance of confirming start, break, lunch and finish times, with an adult, at the beginning of the day. If no times are recorded on the teacher's notes for me, I now write these down on a piece of paper before the children arrive. Recording these transition times in advance, now help me to be organised, ready and informed. This and other sources of practical information and communication, including staff notice boards, emails and word of mouth, if necessary, will help me to know what is going on in that school.

Due to safeguarding reasons, I keep my smartphone in my bag or jacket during lesson time, and only use it during my break or lunchtime. Some schools go so far as to have a strict policy of zero usage, and the phone must be placed in a locker or left in your car all day. Other schools may allow me to show specific photos from my phone, such as when I was a police officer or when I have dressed up in costume for a school dress up day, so long as I have shared those photos with the appropriate member of school leadership for approval first.

Anyone who knows me well, knows how organised I like to be. I like to keep classrooms tidy, and my own study desk at home is meticulously orderly. I rarely lose things, and I like to be punctual for any meeting or appointment. In other words, I always try to do the right thing – even if I mess up! Therefore, I was flabbergasted when, on one occasion, I realised I had inadvertently left my phone in my trouser pocket, and it rang out a song!

This embarrassing scenario happened at a school in early 2019. Being a Catholic school, it would hold a celebration assembly, with prayers, Bible readings, spiritual messages and hymns, every Friday morning. The assembly was a special and spiritual event, and the children always did very well to observe the reverence expected of them.

There were greetings and opening remarks from the headteacher, the lighting of the three candles to represent the Godhead, then a prayer given by the headteacher. There was complete hush among the throng, as almost everyone bowed their heads, and many closed their eyes in anticipation of the prayer being said.

Suddenly, as the headteacher was literally about to utter softly the first words of the prayer, my phone started playing Rockabilly Rebel by Matchbox. I had been listening to this song on the way to work with my phone connected to my handsfree car sound system. My phone was still on full volume! There was a momentary pause in the hall, as I quickly pulled out my phone and switched it off, while the children in my class, sitting just in front of me, whisked their heads around and started giggling at my misfortune. I quietly hastened the children to stop laughing, face the front and bow their heads. Totally embarrassed, I didn't look at the headteacher, but I did say a contrite, "Sorry!" as I meekly bowed my head. Thankfully, no one chastised me then, or even afterwards. They were very considerate despite my awful blunder.

To be informed and aware of key measures and practices for individual children is of great importance. Policies and colleagues will always be my source of information. I recall being tasked with teaching a Year Five class for five weeks. The teacher, I was informed, was ill, and the school had requested me. It was made clear to me by certain staff on the first day, that this particular class was the most difficult in the entire school, in terms of their behaviour. Nevertheless, I remained motivated and accepted the assignment. As I placed my coat in the classroom closet, I noticed a large tub of chocolates on the shelf.

I initially met with the headteacher to discuss the class. He was explicit about what action to take if faced with behaviour issues, including daily updates on the class. I made written notes of this information. Within two days, in consultation with the headteacher and the TA, who worked in the class for one or two lessons a day, I had split up a cluster of boys, most of whom had been sitting near each other and were constantly disturbing others and disrupting the learning. They were a disingenuous group and a real handful! I knew I was up against it and found myself regularly having to report the worst incidents to the necessary adults within the school, including the headteacher. In a very short period of time, I was soon meeting with the parents of some of these boys.

I had also opened the lid of that tub of chocolates on the shelf. My attempts to resist the chocolates were futile and rather pathetic. Feeling guilty but also feeling desperate for some comforting 'chocolate fix' I had eaten one chocolate on the first day. The following day it became a few more chocolates.

The headteacher and senior leadership team, together with other staff, were very sympathetic and supportive. However, I was astounded that one boy named Harvey, whom I felt to be the most difficult, did not have a one-to-one adult to support him. He was an intelligent lad, but unresponsive to instructions and requests. He was also very calculating and showed no remorse when behaving badly. Neither did he recognise that what he was doing was entirely inappropriate and wrong. In other words, Harvey was extremely difficult to control, and the antithesis of good behaviour. Consequently, I made several recommendations that he be given one-to-one support as soon as was possible. Over time, I sensed that my comments about Harvey and some of the other boys, were beginning to frustrate some leadership staff and they were perhaps feeling a sense of hopelessness for these wayward boys, especially Harvey.

Sometimes, no matter what steps and measures are put into place, a child's behaviour can be extremely unbearable. In the third week, Harvey even called a visiting adult, who was giving an informative and enjoyable presentation to the class, a liar. She was appalled, as was I, and told the class that she was shocked by the behaviour from some within the class. After about three weeks of teaching this class, I needed to take a day off sick. I had a heavy virus anyway, but the stress was relentless. I had been pushed too far and was physically and mentally drained. Subsequently, my optimism began to decline. As my energy and enthusiasm began to wane; the number of chocolates continued to dwindle.

I will share just two five-minute snapshots of Harvey's behaviour, to provide a clearer picture of his behaviour. After my day off sick, and upon my recommendations, Harvey was finally given a one-to-one adult, and I felt some relief at this news. During one lesson, his adult support ensured he was settled, but then needed to leave him for a few minutes. No sooner had she left the classroom and closed the door behind her, than he threw his pencil down, walked over to another boy sitting quietly at another table, removed a glove out of the boy's pencil case, placed it on his hand, and proceeded to wander around the classroom prodding others. Harvey ignored the pleadings from the boy who owned the glove, as well as my firm instructions to return the glove and sit down. His support adult, returning earlier than expected, was surprised to find Harvey wandering around, disrupting the peaceful learning environment, while I tried to persuade him back to his seat. Harvey seemed stunned to see her early return too.

On my penultimate day at the school, Harvey's behaviour was so disruptive, that he had to be removed from class in the afternoon. He was returned to class by a member of the senior leadership team at about 3pm. I welcomed him back, noticing that he was watching the adult who brought him back. As soon as she left the classroom, he immediately grabbed a boy by the neck and bent his arm back. He then shoved a girl so hard that she went flying across the room like a bat out of hell. My protests were in vain, so I sent two reliable children to fetch another adult, as the school's policy required. Meanwhile, the miscreant went to a window, which was open for ventilation, tore up a letter he had just been given, dropping the bits of paper onto waiting parents below. He was devious, mischievous and very badly behaved when no other adult was present.

At the end of my final day, I spoke to the class. With a raised voice, I expressed my disappointment and displeasure at the behaviour and attitude of several children in the class. During my lecture and reprimanding, one of the senior members of staff entered the classroom to collect a child. I think she was shocked to hear me reprimanding the children. Nevertheless, I was not deterred and continued my rebuking. There was complete silence - the children were as quiet as mice. The only sound was my raised but controlled voice echoing across the room. Although I singled out the group of difficult boys, especially the most troublesome one, Harvey, from that Year Five class, I had the presence of mind to praise the majority during my diatribe.

Despite applying all the strategies and methods gained from successfully teaching hundreds of classes over the years, as well as being aware of, and adhering to school practices and policy, this class had become one of the most challenging classes I have ever had to work with.

After five long weeks, my assignment was complete. I had given my all and there was nothing more to give. I was void of any spark of desire to stay with that class.

I was depleted. The box of chocolates was now empty.

The teacher, whose class I had covered, was returning to school the following week and would probably assume I was a right greedy so and so for eating all the chocolates, but my reasons were more of an emotional need, rather than just a physical appetite. I had eaten every single chocolate to help fight the day-to-day classroom stresses. I'd certainly put on some weight though, and after five weeks I probably resembled Porky Pig!

Incidentally, I purchased a new tub of chocolates for the teacher with a note of apology.

Several months later, I returned to the same school, but working in a different year group that day. I had assumed that the school would never invite me back, following my struggles with the class, and my raised voice on the final day. Interestingly though, while I was waiting in the playground for the morning bell to sound, every one of the troublesome boys from that Year Five class gathered around me. They were all chatty and seemed overjoyed to see me. They were also very pleasant and polite towards me. Harvey, who you will recall had been the most difficult to control, remained with me while the other boys eventually moved on. I could not believe that he was so friendly to me. It was as though he didn't want to leave my side. Had I made a lasting impression on Harvey and the other boys after all? Had seeds of positivity been planted in their hearts by me? I still wonder to this day.

As previously discussed, showing support to colleagues at an assigned school, especially when they are trying to enforce policies, rules, procedures and routines, is good practice. I believe we can set a bad precedent when we don't always follow through with school or classroom rules, and we must be careful not to allow the children to rule, govern and dictate to adults. Nevertheless, there have been occasions when I have chosen to use discretion instead.

I recall a cherished moment, while teaching a Year Five class in Bournemouth in autumn 2019. They were a class I had taught previously, so I was abreast of their abilities. After sharing the learning, and assigning the differentiated written task to each child, I reminded the children of my expectations. Not only were the children required to construct differentiated sentences using various forms of grammatical inclusion, but the number of sentences they had to record were also differentiated. A few children were required to write five sentences, others ten, while the higher ability children needed to write more than ten. In addition, I told the class, that if they did not complete their sentences, they would have to finish them during breaktime – a policy within class that I was aware of.

After a few minutes, I noticed that one boy called Anton, was constantly talking, rather than focusing on his learning. I made it clear to him what the consequences would be if he did not complete his work, and also offered him some assistance. He promised to stop talking and work hard.

A short while later, Anton was silently crying at his table. I approached his table and asked if he was okay. He told me he found writing very difficult and did not think he could complete all ten sentences in the allocated time frame. Crouching down by his table, I quietly told him that as long as he did not distract others on his table, and if he completed seven sentences in the time left, I would permit him to go outside to play. "Thank you, Mr Kersey!" he said.

"Do you promise me, Anton?" I asked.

"Yes, I won't talk. I'll do my best!" he assured me.

"Then don't worry. I'll check your work at the end of the lesson but don't forget to ask me for help, if you get stuck," I reassured him.

Anton got to work and said not a word to the other children around him. At the end of the lesson, he came to me and sheepishly said, "I have only done six sentences, Mr Kersey." I could sense his nervousness and worry.

"Anton, you didn't complete seven?" I gently asked.

"Yes, I know. I really tried," he said sadly.

Looking him in the eye, I continued, "I know you did Anton. I was watching you. You weren't chatting and you were working hard. You have done your best Anton. You'll be able to go out to play."

He was thrilled. He gently leant his head against my upper

arm and said, "Thank you, Mr Kersey."

The classroom rule may have been to keep a child in at breaktime, in order to complete their learning. I had done just that with this particular class on a number of occasions. However, in Anton's case, I felt otherwise. Every so often, even when I am informed and aware, I will also use my discretion to make an informed decision. In my opinion, that is good teaching. That is the power of teacher discretion. That is the power of teacher compassion.

Teaching, as a profession, is constantly changing. It isn't always exciting, but it is always evolving. The sad reality though, is that teaching is sometimes portrayed in a negative light. I recall watching the ITV Good Morning Britain show on the 22nd of January 2019. The presenters, including Piers Morgan, were excited about the 24th National Television Awards that evening. They were hoping to win one of the categories. A viewer had sent a text message that morning, expressing his love of the show in comparison to the opposition. He stated how the morning show on the other channel, the BBC, was like waking up to your teacher. That made me chuckle, yet I wondered why he would regard waking up to his teacher as a 'boring' thing. There is an underlying trend here, which I would like to touch upon.

I'll admit that some people in society see teaching as boring, tedious and mundane. Nevertheless, from the viewpoint of a primary school teacher, I have experienced the opposite. There is a certain amount of monotony with teaching. It isn't always amazing and thrilling! The days and weeks can sometimes feel like they are dragging on and on. However, responsibility and expectation assume a degree of autonomy, and I have seen colleagues working tirelessly to fulfil deadlines and commitments. These dedicated teachers, work hard to produce interesting, creative and informative lessons. Yes, there will be students who will be uninterested in certain subjects. The reality is that no teacher will be able to please and engage every child in every lesson and activity, every day.

Teachers spend quality time with children of all abilities, but especially with those who are struggling. They are fair, creative and open-minded. They give up their hours after school to run clubs, meet with concerned parents, and attend various meetings. Often, they sacrifice their brief lunch period in order to run a lunchtime club too. I believe there needs to be more favourable, supportive and positive talk of teachers. It is deplorable that all too often they receive minimal acknowledgement and gratitude from certain sections of the media and society. They deserve the praise, and society needs to elevate teaching more. A good teacher knows their children, as well as their subjects, and they work ridiculously hard to achieve amazing results for the children. Teachers deserve better recognition!

Furthermore, HLTAs and TAs are an incredibly significant resource at school, and I have had the privilege of working with countless numbers of these professionals over the years, who have largely been fantastic colleagues. On many occasions they have reassured me during some difficult and challenging situations. The

HLTAs and TAs, include Sarah Webb, who I wish to add was probably the best TA I have ever worked with, Trisha, Sharna, Katy, Suhaila, Jenny and Sue. These and so many other HLTAs and TAs have been a joy to work with and have all been great team players too!

Some people, other than educators, may be surprised to hear that the roles of a HLTA and TA has changed significantly in recent years. Too many of them are now expected to work in their own time at home, to prepare resources or complete other work assigned to them by the school. These educators, as with teachers, are also under pressure and feel a heavy weight from their expanding responsibilities. There isn't always an increase in pay for the extra working hours either. Many cover for the teacher when the teacher is absent - again without necessarily receiving an increase in their daily rate. I am sure the majority of schools would wish to pay their HLTAs and TAs a more generous wage, but tight school budgets can make that problematic.

I have the utmost respect for full-time teachers, part-time teachers, teaching assistants, school leadership and fellow supply teachers. I used to tease my wife, who has been teaching full-time for thirty years now, that teachers had it easy with all their holidays. That was until the realisation of the sheer amount of work she was undertaking each day dawned on me, like some kind of epiphany. There was no more joking after that. My blasé attitude was replaced with the greatest admiration and appreciation for her and all educators. The full awareness hit me even harder when I qualified as a teacher years later. If I had been 'hit by a truck' beforehand at the level of teacher workload, then as a full-time teacher, I was 'struck head-on by a 'steam train' racing at full speed. That 'steam train workload' wouldn't stop to pause at stations either. It just kept relentlessly going and going and going, and for some educators, it will be full-on - until they and their 'steam train' eventually crash! Educators may be superheroes without capes, but they are vulnerable too.

Lesson 4

Vulnerability

Help!

Each of us are gifted with talents, gifts and strengths. We may take pride in our experiences, knowledge and achievements, and naturally can be set in our opinions when conversing with others. We say to ourselves that we have experienced life, studied hard for excellent qualifications, travelled, read and researched, and subsequently we are educated and our views of the world, therefore, must be aired because we are right. Every opinion does indeed matter and I am not suggesting that one needs to change a time held conviction or way of life. Some principles and beliefs should remain forged in your heart when you feel they are absolutely right to you, no matter the pressure from others. Nevertheless, 'no one is an island' and from time to time, especially when we are faced with the unknown or a plethora of seemingly insurmountable obstacles, we need the approach, advice and help from other people and sources, no matter how learned we are, or how strong we may feel.

When others are reaching out to us, it may be natural to at first feel a sense of steely grit. We may be self-assured in our own abilities to cope alone and move forward. Other times, we may hesitate and feel embarrassed, vulnerable, uncertain, inadequate and even fearful of the unknown. Self-doubt creeps in and before we know it, we may 'bury our head in the sand' hoping that the challenging barrier in front of us will somehow disappear into thin air.

For any supply teacher, it is the unknown that can present one of the greatest challenges. Whether teaching at a new school, meeting new staff and children, learning new routines and teaching methods or arriving late and 'hitting the ground running' I must be willing to quickly adapt to the learning environment and accept support when necessary. I must do it with an air of confidence but equal unpretentiousness. In line with this attitude, I love this quote from Stephen R. Covey.

"The person who is truly effective has the humility and reverence to recognize his own perceptual limitations and to appreciate the rich resources available through interaction with the hearts and minds of other human beings."[7]

The greater my aptitude, the more effective part I will play in the education machine. Having sound subject knowledge will increase my confidence to teach, and will help to dissipate any initial anxiety, both of which will contribute to a harmonious atmosphere. When I lack confidence or knowledge in a particular area, I research that subject. I strive constantly to increase my subject knowledge and to improve my skills, which inevitably contributes to a less stressful, and more fluent and enjoyable class experience. Knowledge really is power.

Notwithstanding this, I don't know the answers to everything, and the best source of information within a school, as already mentioned, are the adults. Even so, I don't underestimate the 'bright buttons' in my classrooms either. They too might be able to answer any queries I have. I always keep in mind that, depending upon the age group, there may be a child in the class who knows more than me about a given subject. If I make a mistake with a teaching point, I always avoid going on the defensive and taking it personally. There have been plenty of occasions, especially in my first year or two of supplying, when I made a teaching error in an Upper Key Stage Two class, and perhaps incorrectly taught a calculation or concept. Often, it was a child who pointed out the error. Whenever I make a mistake, and a child points it out, I often apply some humour, responding with something like, "Yes, I knew that. I was just testing you all. Well done for paying attention. You can have a house point." Children laugh and other adults in the room enjoy the joke too. I praise the child who corrected me and reward them for noticing the obvious oversight.

Children can be charming angels, and we all know they can be extremely challenging at times. Some days, I succeed with a class, while other days I may feel I have really struggled. Here is a little poem I wrote in 2021 which humorously depicts both scenarios.

"Frequently, I am Mary Poppins!
I enter the classroom
Sprinkled magic envelopes

Children are inspired
Children are in awe
Success follows
And the day is truly delightful!

Occasionally, I am Mr Bean!
I enter the classroom
Sprinkled magic evaporates
Children are tired
Children are in uproar
Failure follows
And the day is truly dreadful!"
- By Grant J. Kersey
18th September 2021

Even for the best teachers, the second stanza describes perfectly what it can feel like on some days. That is teaching – it is a pressured world! I have had my fair share of difficult classes, and it is often during such difficult experiences that our character and resolve is tested to the extreme. I wish to share a few of the more challenging teaching experiences, where despite being regarded by my agency as a strong teacher, I actually felt out of my depth in 'deep water' and struggled to 'keep afloat.'

In January 2020, I found myself with yet another difficult class. One of the owners of the agency had rung me, and told me

Lesson 4 - Vulnerability - Help!

he had met a headteacher at a Headteachers' Conference, who had recently been appointed to work at a struggling school. The new headteacher had taken on this role, while simultaneously overseeing two other primary schools, when the current headteacher had been taken ill. I came to know the new Headteacher as an exceptional Executive Headteacher. She was one of the best I have ever had the privilege to work with in education.

In their discussions, the headteacher had told my boss that she needed cover for a mixed Year Five/Six class with only twelve children on the register. However, their teacher had been sick for some time, and the resultant lack of continuity had caused the children to be somewhat unsettled. Their supply teacher would need to nurture them, while at the same time introduce clear classroom boundaries. Those words were a clear signal to me that these children would be a challenging bunch!

The school was situated in the gorgeous New Forest. There was no playground, and the public fields opposite the school served as the children's play area. Neither was there a school hall, so lunch was therefore held in two of the three classrooms. It was a diminutive school within an idyllic setting.

There is the tendency for some parents to believe that their child would do so much better in a little village school, but the reality is that these tiny schools tend to have less funding than the larger schools. Thus, small budgets frequently mean fewer resources and less supporting staff. On the other hand, these small village schools can have some of the happiest of school environments for children.

Lesson 4 - Vulnerability - Help!

After an initial meeting with the headteacher, I commenced my new assignment. It soon became apparent, that despite the relatively small number of children in the class, my initial thoughts were correct - they were indeed going to be a handful! Teaching mixed aged classes is always an extra challenge anyway, but this small group of children were something else. Every day, there were frequent behavioural issues, such as insolence, rudeness, bickering, negativity, increased and persistent noise level, backchat, disruption, bullying and deceit. Most of the children behaved in this way and dealing with them alone - without an adult supporting in class -often left me mentally depleted at the end of the day. Nevertheless, I looked for positives, and when asked by parents or staff how my day had been, I tried to remain optimistic and constructive. I am a great believer in focusing on the good that a child does, and I acknowledge any improvements no matter how slight. The praise is always from the heart. Nevertheless, if there had been an outrageous moment, I would need to mention it in confidence to the specific parent, or perhaps to a colleague such as the headteacher.

Each day was a new day, and so I persevered. I complimented the children, guided them, corrected them and rewarded them. Quite simply, I loved them. One distinct lesson, which was always the most strenuous to maintain control over the class, was physical education! In all settings prior to a PE lesson, I always remind the children of my expectations and clear instructions while still in the classroom, and I would repeat these expectations again when we have arrived at the setting for the activity. PE at this school though was made even more challenging because the sessions were held at a local village hall. The class had to travel a very short distance by minibus in order to get there. During my checks on the minibus, one girl regularly told me to shut up when I asked her to put her seat belt on, and during the lesson, some ran around ignoring instructions, while others went to hide in the kitchen. Sometimes, children stormed outside so that I could not see them, hid behind the stage curtain, or screamed, bickered and cried because someone had cheated during the activity or game. Although this kind of behaviour occurred every day in class, PE lessons in the village hall were by far the most stressful and fraught. It was an absolute nightmare situation and filled with copious challenges for me.

Each week, I would need to firmly and verbally reprimand several children in the village hall, and they would have to face the consequences of their poor choices back at school. I often threatened the entire class with no PE lesson for the following week, but I felt that that would only punish the few well-behaved children, who would miss out on their deserved PE lesson.

I continued to remain upbeat and worked hard to make all my lessons, in the classroom and at the village hall, interesting and engaging. On one occasion, I brought in items of police uniform, such as my old helmet, a cap and a truncheon. They loved wearing either the cap or helmet, or both! At the end of each day, they would eagerly anticipate a new police story from me. It was a great way to allow them into my life and connect with them. There were never any 'blood and gore' stories shared, but sadly, those police stories came to an abrupt end, after the headteacher informed me that the parents of a particularly sensitive child had complained to her parents because one story had frightened her. I decided to stop telling any of my stories, just in case. I didn't mention who had complained, but the class were clearly disappointed. They really did enjoy those stories.

Over time, I successfully transformed the behaviour of most of the class. The majority began to respond to me each day, and a few, who had been difficult in the early days, began to be more considerate, polite and grateful towards me, as were their parents. One girl, named Belinda, who managed to greatly improve her behaviour over the seven or so weeks that I was there, even gave me a handwritten card after I had been at the school for a couple of weeks. What was so significant to me was not just the apology, but her thoughtful words, "I am trying to improve my behaviour." Are we not all trying to improve in life? The key to improving our lives is recognising how and where we have failed and making the necessary adjustments. I was so proud of Belinda for recognising her failings and for her desire to be a better person. She even kindly added a pack of chocolate wafers for me, which didn't last very long!

Lesson 4 - Vulnerability - Help!

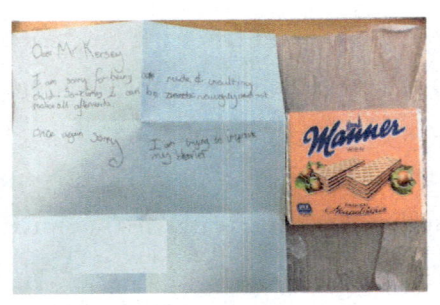

Belinda's handwritten note

Conversely, two children, named Ella and Tyler, remained very stubborn and obstinate. They were not friends with each other and would tease each other most days. Every day, I worked hard to keep them apart, and would frequently need to speak to their respective parents. I tried my best to keep a fair balance, so the feedback would occasionally be heartening, even if it was sometimes still a little concerning.

One day, a few children gave me some useful feedback concerning the changes I had introduced. The comments went like this.

Girl 1
Mr Kersey, the class never spoke unkindly to Mr (name removed) or other supply teachers the way they speak to you.

Girl 2
That's because we have discipline now.
Before, we could do what we wanted.

Girl 3
Yeah, and we're learning so much more with Mr Kersey.

Boy 1:
You're doing a good job Mr Kersey!

Wow! Hearing such positive comments from a few of the children, some of whom themselves had initially been very difficult to handle, gave me another dose of hope. I continued to press forward each day. From my experiences of teaching thousands of children, I toiled long and hard to show the entire class the level of love, support, understanding and discipline, which they needed. The change in attitude by some of the children in the class, from being self-centred to seeing a situation from another's viewpoint, plus the incredible headteacher and her supportive team, and several appreciative parents, who often thanked me for what I was trying to achieve for the children, kept me motivated and moving ahead – and teachers need to hear this when they are up against it! Nonetheless, some children persisted in putting up barriers each day. I had no intention of breaking down those barriers straight away, but I did want to remove them gradually, 'brick by brick.' Sometimes, it felt as though when one brick was removed, two or three bricks were added to that wall. Ella and Tyler in particular, continued to build even higher and stronger barriers. I began to feel mentally exhausted!

In spite of that, I didn't complain to my agency. In my seven years with the agency, there have only been a handful of times when I have complained to them about an issue at school. Largely, when faced with problems, I have kept the situation quiet and resolved the matter with the school. After several weeks, as I was leaving school one day, Carrie, the office lady muttered to me, "I don't know how you do it Grant!" I told her that I genuinely loved, understood and cared for the children, and some of them now felt this because there was zero pretence from me. Yet most days, I would leave school feeling slaughtered, only to optimistically return the next day. Hope kept me going!

One day however, I did not return to school. It was a Wednesday. The previous day had been so difficult, so desperate and demanding, that as I drove home alone on the Tuesday, and with the windows fully wound up and music blasting from the car sound system, I screamed and swore at the top of my voice in pain and frustration. I continued this emotional response for several minutes as I manoeuvred down an almost empty country lane. I did not want anyone to hear my anger and pleas for help. I swore at the injustice and unfairness I was experiencing, as well as the repeated deceit, spite and selfishness I encountered within the class.

Everyone has a breaking point if pushed too far, and as Mahatma Gandhi put it, "The world has enough for everyone's need, but not enough for everyone's greed."[8]

A normally strong, stable and upright man was having a mental breakdown. On numerous occasions as a supply teacher, I had stood at a mental precipice and an emotional cliff edge. This was different. Now I stared down into the abyss, with a sense of futility and failure. Leaning forward, I felt like I had toppled over the edge this time. That evening, I did not tell a soul, not even my wife. I chose to hide my pain and suffered alone. I was rendered silent. It is only now, while writing this, that I have chosen to reveal some of the innermost suffering I felt at the time. Mentally, I felt like fragile glass having been pounded by rocks and stones, then unsympathetically trampled underfoot and kicked to a forgotten corner.

The next morning, I lay on my bed, mentally shattered and emotionally broken. I was totally crushed! The many afflictions I had suffered, as a result of some extremely difficult behaviours over seven years as a supply teacher, now culminated in this most challenging of classes. It was now taking its toll on me mentally, to an even greater depth than I had ever experienced previously. The pain swirled around my mind as I recalled innumerable injustices I had encountered, not just at this school but at other schools – and even in my life! I had to fight the mental pain with every sinew, muscle and bone in my body, as I lay flat on my back staring up at the ceiling. I was conflicted!

The desire to help those children and educators was at the back of my mind, and a determining factor in returning to work. Mustering up great inner resolve, strength, determination and positivity to return to that class, I dragged myself back to school that same morning. I had taken one day off work, but so easily could have rested and recouped for a month or more. As I arrived at school, I 'painted a smile' on my face – but any observant individual could probably see the hurt in my eyes.

One problem with being a popular supply teacher is you become the number one choice for many schools. In addition, my agency knew of my strengths and skills, and the success rate I had achieved while working with extremely troublesome and challenging children. When a tough job came in, I would inevitably be called upon. It is often the same for full-time teachers. Senior leadership will recognise a good teacher who can sustain discipline within the classroom, and also teach effectively. Invariably, they send the children with challenges to that teacher for the year. Consequently, the behaviour is so extreme and frequent that the teacher may begin to struggle. Senior leadership decide that the teacher cannot cope and may then question their ability to teach. The teacher then feels exploited and unappreciated. It's a cycle that I have often come across in a number of schools.

However, it is not just teachers and supporting staff who feel the tremendous strain. Headteachers and leadership are under the microscope too. There is intense pressure on them from all corners. In one corner is the government, local authority, agencies and Ofsted inspectors, who sometimes scrutinise rather than support. They are accountable to the school governors from another corner and have performance management targets to meet themselves. Then there is the education, welfare and safeguarding of the children to meet, as well as the high expectations from parents. Finally, they have the needs of their staff, whom they have a duty of care for, including workload pressures, mental health and wellbeing. Headteachers feel obligated to appease the deadlines and demands from all sides, as they constantly try and strike a balance. You'd have to be someone special to be a headteacher in today's world with all its immediate demands and high expectations.

To me, however, this particular class was much more than a tough job, and represented a microcosm of much that is wrong

Lesson 4 - Vulnerability - Help!

in modern society: laziness, ignorance, indifference, impatience, refusal to take responsibility for one's own actions, bullying, barefaced lies, division and hatred.

When faced with such extremely difficult children, I am able to 'feel' for them. Children who have emotional challenges resonate with me. I have a wave of compassion and sympathy for them, and I am sensitive to their needs when they feel unbelieved, useless, rejected, despised, anxious, detached, discouraged, frustrated and angry. I do it out of love, empathy and understanding because of what I personally suffered in my childhood. My 'wounds' have taught me to soothe others – children and adults, with their own pain. Regarding the extreme adversities in my childhood, being magnanimous has brought me tremendous peace. You can let your past destroy you, or you can let it develop you. The choice is yours!

On the day I returned to school, Ella, the most laborious girl in the class, was having another fretful day. Although she was settled on arrival at school, she soon became agitated as other children came in and early morning assignments were given. She gave no reason for her refusal to cooperate. When a friend of hers kindly placed a whiteboard and pen on the table they shared, Ella swiped them onto the floor, together with a textbook and some papers. Ella then refused to pick the items up so another child offered to retrieve them. While I was trying to deal with Ella's misbehaviour, I was simultaneously trying to engage with a parent at the classroom door, who had asked to speak with me there and then. Parents want to talk at the most inopportune moment sometimes.

Lesson 4 - Vulnerability - Help!

As the morning progressed, Ella's behaviour worsened, and she became embroiled in a number of spiteful accusations with other children. It seemed to me that Ella was initiating most of these battles, and although I moved a couple of children to another area of the classroom to try to quell the situation, and implemented other management techniques, all my attempts to reason with Ella and encourage her failed. These constant interruptions of bad behaviour in the classroom, especially since there was no second adult to provide additional support, were very frustrating and disruptive, not just for me as the teacher, but also for the children who wanted to learn and were trying to focus.

A little later, there was a heated argument between Ella and another girl during a maths lesson. I invited Ella to move elsewhere, even out of the classroom if it would help her, but she declined. Thankfully, the other girl was willing to move, but before long, I saw that Ella was assiduously writing notes. This was a maths lesson yet from where I stood, I could see she was writing a series of sentences and paragraphs. I sensed that she was reporting incidents or verbal communications she found upsetting, and I asked to see her notes and offered her support again, but she declined support and refused to show me her notes.

By the end of the lesson, she had completed none of the maths work assigned to her, in spite of my constant offers of help. I picked up her written notes. In her notes, there was no mention of her misdemeanours and blatant disregard for following instructions that morning. Neither had she mentioned about her teasing a boy and girl because of their 'romantic' friendship in class, which had greatly upset both children, who had felt embarrassed and self-conscious by Ella's mocking comments. There was no mention either, of the patience and kindness I had shown her. Nor was it noted down, the number of times I tried to encourage her with offers of help with her maths task.

Instead, she had claimed to be the victim of harassment that morning and how she had reported certain incidents of bullying and intimidation to me, during the maths lesson, and that I had totally ignored her. I reminded her of the several occasions that I had intervened during any disagreements and teasing with other children that morning. I then asked her why she had not told me about these other matters, which had apparently upset her during the lesson. She said that the SENDco had told her to write things down and not tell me. With that, she stood up, and ran out of the class, screaming and loudly crying to her mum, Annette, who was working at the school as a TA with another class. I could see her mum consoling her in the corridor. Just great! I thought. That's all I need after what I have struggled with recently.

Equally concerning, was the fact that I could not understand why the SENDco would advise a child to go behind her teacher's back, rather than confide in him so that he could help the children to resolve their differences in the moment. Additionally, there were comments about me in Ella's notes that simply were not true. I had dealt with all concerns which she had informed me of. I was livid that half-truths and lies had been said about me!

Lesson 4 - Vulnerability - Help!

I approached Annette, lifting my arm with the notes in my hand, and said, "I'm not happy about this. I'd like to talk to you about it at lunch time please." I was firm and direct but did not raise my voice. Annette looked a little confused, but responded, "Okay."

At the first opportunity, I reported the incident to the headteacher. I was clear that the SENDco was wrong to go behind my back, and she agreed that it had not necessarily been the most appropriate advice to give to Ella. She offered to join my discussion with Annette at lunch time, but I declined as I did not want the meeting to be perceived as an official, formal meeting.

At lunchtime, as I headed to the staff room, I saw Annette. She seemed calm but unsure about meeting me during the lunch break. I suggested we could meet after school if she preferred, but she gave me no definitive answer.

As I was eating my lunch, a colleague walked in and asked the staff, "What's wrong with Annette? She looks a little tearful." I felt dreadful! I realised that I had taken out my frustration on Annette, who had done nothing wrong. I had left her upset and distressed, and I knew that I needed to apologise for the abrupt way I had spoken to her. I was conscious that Annette was in an awkward position as both a TA at the school, and a mother trying to support her very disruptive daughter. She was receiving almost daily reports about Ella's rude and bad behaviour, and I could only imagine how she must have agonised over Ella's struggles while continuing to concentrate on her own role at the school. It must have been a

Lesson 4 - Vulnerability - Help!

difficult conflict of interests for her.

A wave of compassion came over me now that I saw the situation from Annette's perspective. I was determined to try to make amends, and console her, whatever her response proved to be.

When I found Annette, I could see that she had obviously been crying. I called her name and said gently, "I'm so sorry for the way I spoke to you. I was abrupt and shouldn't have spoken that way. The situation must be very difficult for you. There's no need for us to meet unless you want to." She softly thanked me. I gave a reassuring smile and walked away. I shared this with the headteacher who was pleased with this outcome.

I had been offended, not by Annette of course, but by what I saw as Ella's false comments, and by the SENDco apparently going behind my back. In hindsight, I could see that the SENDco was likely just trying to find solutions to Ella's concerns. It certainly took humility and courage for me to apologise. It would have been easy for me to have justified my reaction, but I had upset Annette, and needed to do all I could to make the situation right. If I had been too stubborn to apologise, an otherwise healthy working relationship could easily have been jeopardised. In fact, although Ella's behaviour did not improve, my relationship with Annette positively thrived, and I was grateful to her for forgiving my moment of agitation. It is important to be humble, yet courageous enough to make the right call, when faced with a disagreement and upset with a colleague.

The class, on the whole, did continue to improve, both academically and behaviourally. The children, generally, were grateful to me, and remarked that they didn't want me to leave. Parents too, made similar comments. Then, in my final week at this school, I received a gift of a braided wristband from a girl in another class who lived in a care home and had behavioural challenges. As she tied it to my wrist, she said, "Mr Kersey, I made this especially for you 'cos you are my friend."

I had often seen this girl at breaktime, lunchtime and around school, and would try and spare a moment with her. Just like the story of Greg, previously shared, I would ask how her day was going, complement and praise her small steps of good behaviour. I had no idea that I had made such a positive and healthy impact on this child from another class - until that day!

I had once again faced a very challenging situation; this time during a transitional period for the children and the school, but had gratefully come out on top. I had remained resolute to meet the objectives I was set at the beginning of my seven-week tenure at the school: to help the children to feel cared for and set clear classroom rules and boundaries to assist with their learning and behaviour. That I had achieved – for almost every child!

Nearing the end of my tenure at this school, I was approached by one of the owners of the agency again, to accept a long-term, maternity leave assignment at a superb primary school. I had always enjoyed my assignments there because the headteacher, leadership and staff, had always made me feel welcomed at the school. In addition, the organisation within the school gave me an impression of being very purposeful, and there were high standards and expectations, which seem to run smoothly like clockwork. The school produced excellent results year after year, and the behaviour of the children was overwhelmingly exceptional. However, for some reason, I felt uneasy about accepting this appointment. Something inside me was telling me not to accept the job. I shared my concerns with my wife, and she told me to, "Go with your gut feeling! You have never been wrong when you do."

Accordingly, I declined the offer and thought that was the end of the matter. However, my boss was persistent, and when he rang me a few days later, I sensed some urgency in his voice. He explained that the headteacher, named James, a wonderful man, whom I knew well, was in a desperate situation. Due to the previous candidate pulling out of the teaching position, he was left in a quandary. There was still no one to fill the post, and with the class teacher going on maternity leave in a matter of weeks, there was a pressing need for cover.

My boss said that my name had been mentioned, and as I listened to him, I felt some concern for James and his situation. Finally, despite retaining that uneasy feeling, I agreed to meet with James.

At our meeting, James informed me that if I agreed to provide cover, my assignment would include supporting two other teachers, one of whom was a newly qualified teacher (NQT), called Sally. The other, called Hannah, was in her second year of teaching. I enquired about planning, and he reassured me that all the required planning was in place, and my role would mainly involve reassuring these new teachers, and supporting them in challenging situations, such as dealing with difficult parents. I explained that I still had to finish my current assignment at the small village school where the regular class teacher was doing a phased return to full-time work. James offered me two weeks' part-time work at this school, enabling me to complete my commitment at the other school, before starting at his school full-time. I then accepted the assignment.

    My eyes were soon opened to the mountain of work expected of me within just a few days. I met with Suzie, the teacher whose class I would be covering, on the Friday before I was to start the following Monday. She took three quarters of an hour simply to explain the reading routines that had been established, apologetically enumerating each of the requirements. Then she hit me with a bombshell. The school was expecting an Ofsted visit, and the main focus of which would be reading!

    Due to this anticipated visit, the school had recently implemented a requirement that teachers should read with at least three children before taking the morning register. This exercise included writing detailed notes on each of these children at the same time. Suzie told me that she had found this task difficult to accomplish. As you can imagine, children take a little while putting personal items, such as coats, bags, lunchboxes and water bottles away when they first arrive. Some delay settling down to their morning task, which, invariably needs to be explained several times, as children enter the classroom at different times. Plus, listening to any parents who wish to talk, or a colleague who comes in to pass on a message, or a number of children who surround you because they have a sudden urge to want to share something with you. I could just envisage the practical challenges with this task from leadership. Knowing this, I wondered how many children Suzie had managed to listen to that week. "Just one," she said. "There simply isn't time in the morning before registration." Concerned, I asked her why the school had placed these new and difficult demands on the teachers. "Because of Ofsted," she replied. This seemed entirely unreasonable to me, and I said rather flippantly, "So it's okay to implement all these new ideas and programmes in readiness for an Ofsted visit, but no one considers the extra burden and stress on teachers!"

"But we have to get ready for Ofsted, Mr Kersey. That's why!" said Suzie.

"I understand that Suzie," I replied. "I just wish I'd been told about Ofsted when I met with James."

For me, it wasn't the actual Ofsted visit that concerned me, but rather the extra workload inevitably imposed on teachers while 'waiting' for the inspection. I've seen this occur many times in schools, in the weeks and months prior to an expected Ofsted inspection, and it is normally the teachers who bear the brunt of these often unreasonable and extra work demands.

From time to time, leadership may introduce new ideas following pressure from the government, outside agencies, parents, and even their own staff. Occasionally, staff are not given enough time to embed these new routines and practices before indecision kicks in and they are changed again. Consequently, the policy or idea can sometimes not be fully implemented by staff because it may either have not been thought through properly by leadership, or time has not been allocated sufficiently – though it all looks good on paper when Ofsted does visit! The staff, and most often the teachers, can then feel demoralised and discouraged. In other words, it's the ground level staff who do all the running around and grafting, with very little appreciation and praise from the powers that be. When a school is graded 'outstanding' or 'good' by Ofsted, you can be sure it's those teachers who have done most of the hard miles in order to achieve this success.

The extra obligations in the daily routines became more and more apparent as each day went by. The staff, and particularly Hannah and Sally, were dedicated, gracious and warm. They worked enormously hard every day, and it was not unusual for several teachers to remain at school until about 6pm. Some would have remained there longer, but the custom was for the site manager to sound the alarm bell just before 6pm, as a little reminder to the teachers and leadership to hurry up and go home! The challenge for me this time was not the children, who were delightful, or a clash of personalities with a colleague, who were all superb. On this occasion, it was purely the intense workload.

During one private moment, one of the teachers from another year group, shared her thoughts. "I've worked in a few other schools in the area, and I have never been as busy as I am here. There's so much more work here than I've experienced before." Everyone was extremely busy.

In addition to teaching, I was required to attend weekly staff meetings and other meetings after school, which is unusual for supply teachers. I spoke to Hannah and shared with her what the headteacher had told me about the planning already being in place. To my surprise she disappointingly said, "That would be nice but there is no planning saved from previous years because last year was a bit chaotic and a mess. What was saved was not good enough to use this year so we have to do the planning from scratch each week."

One day, we held an impromptu planning meeting after school, led by Hannah. It had been a typically hectic day and we were all tired. During the meeting, I reiterated that I was not totally confident with the process of planning, which is not something generally required of supply teachers. Although I am competent with technology, I was not conversant with the best up-to-date programmes and websites I needed to find. My lack of up-to-date knowledge in this area meant that I was much slower at completing planning tasks than my colleagues, and I felt I needed some guidance and training. After the meeting, I looked at Hannah. She was rubbing her eyes which were red and moist. There were delicate tears trickling down both cheeks. She gently commented, as though somewhat surprised, "Oh, I have tears!"

I sensed she felt overburdened, but I said, "Is that because you're tired?" "No," she replied. "I just feel overwhelmed with the responsibility of being the year leader."

I suppose the realisation of her new role, with its adjacent expectations and increase in responsibilities was sinking in. I felt great empathy for her. Here was a teacher, only halfway through her second year, being asked to be the new Year Leader. Sally jokingly remarked, "We're like the blind leading the blind!" Yes, that we were I thought.

I continued to really struggle with the workload. The daily tasks and expectations were just incredible, with almost every minute being accounted for. Furthermore, there was also an urgency for getting all the test papers marked during test week. Plus, the test scores needed to be recorded online, together with the age-related score for each child. There were numerous daily child and classroom routines to remember, and frequent meetings. I was not used to all these extra tasks and obligations as a supply teacher.

Had I been on a full-time teacher's pay, then perhaps I could have accepted the workload better. Instead, I was on a meagre supply teacher's pay, and it seemed unreasonable to expect a supply teacher to take on the work of a full-time teacher, and then some, without receiving the equivalent pay. This concerned me more and more!

For the first time, in spite of the many challenges I had faced previously in my seven years as a supply teacher, I had discovered my limitation, and although my colleagues were enormously supportive, I found myself falling behind with the marking and other tasks within a couple of weeks.

Once again, I felt conflicted between my desire to remain at the school and help during their challenging time, and the struggle I faced.

Additionally, I felt that I was holding the team back: a glitch in an otherwise well-oiled machine. I needed to discuss my concerns with someone, so I sent two text messages to the agency in the space of a few days, asking for someone to call me to discuss my concerns. I received no response to either text message, and yet I really needed to talk to someone. In desperation, I sent a third text on the following Monday morning while sat in my car, saying, "Good morning (name of agency owner), I won't be staying at (name of school). The workload, meetings, planning, and so on, are far greater than I originally anticipated. The pay does not match the workload, which will just increase over the coming weeks. They really need an experienced teacher to support the NQT and the other teacher, who is only in her second year of teaching. I did message you twice last week to discuss this but heard nothing from you."

It appeared that the school had been made aware of this third text message to my agency, because one of the deputy heads named Betty, came into my classroom that morning, while I was setting up for the day. She asked how I was. I was upbeat and tried to be positive once again, but this time I felt the inclination to also be upfront with her. I told her that I was struggling with the workload, and to my surprise, as I thought she would be disappointed with me, she was very sympathetic. As the children were soon to

Lesson 4 - Vulnerability - Help!

arrive, we agreed to meet a little later.

At breaktime, I found Betty in her office. We chatted, and I opened up to her and shared my concerns. She listened and reassured me. The fact that I had received very little ICT training during all my supply years was becoming taxing for me. I told her that I felt a burden to the team and was holding them back because I was not totally adept at using ICT for planning, and this slowed me down during Planning, Preparation and Assessment time (PPA). I was like a Championship footballer being signed up by a top flight Premiership Club. I was out of my league, but I was modest enough to admit this.

Betty was amazing! She put my fears to rest and reassured me that she would personally train me in ICT in order for me to be au fait with the latest technology. She also offered me what the school called PPA Plus. This gave the staff an extra couple of hours per week, out of class, to plan, mark work, or prepare resources. This would compensate for my attendance at staff meetings.

I had genuine issues and concerns, yet I was willing to learn. I was teachable! I happily agreed to both offers of help and support. Betty then offered me a chocolate Bourbon biscuit from her jar. She was known for her chocolate Bourbon biscuit jar, and any member of staff who needed a chocolate fix went to Betty's office and helped themselves! Even while we were talking, a Year Five teacher came in and took a couple of biscuits from the jar.

Clearly, that moment in Betty's office was not about chocolate Bourbons. It was about someone who was sincerely interested in supporting me. I felt she had resolved my concerns, which suddenly dissipated. Someone had taken the time to listen to me. I needed to hear those encouraging words because I was faced with a 'mountain to climb' at the school, with the workload and my ICT limitations, but that brief encounter with one of the deputy heads lifted my spirits.

Suddenly, I began to believe in myself again. I had a renewed sense of optimism, and I was ready and raring to go forward. I knew I could do this, and was determined to stay and support the school, and more importantly, my team. Hannah and Sally were two dedicated and inspirational colleagues, despite being fairly new to full-time teaching. They were two of the loveliest teachers I have ever had the pleasure to work with. No question, query or help, no matter how stupid or repetitive it may have seemed to me, was too much to ask of them. Despite my limitations, they made me feel welcome. They made me feel wanted.

I was able to speak to my boss over the phone that evening, and informed him that I was going to see this assignment through to the end. However, I wanted reassurances that my daily pay rate would increase. He seemed to understand my situation and asked me to leave it with him while he considered what to do about the pay.

What did I learn from this challenging experience? I learnt that the most effective management comes from building relationships, and then knowing how best to approach a problem or issue. This applied to Betty at this school. She made me feel that there was someone who would carefully listen to my concerns and apply immediate steps to assist me. Making mistakes, or in this case, feeling a lack of confidence in a specific area, and then looking at solutions to these issues, is growth mindset. I didn't hide from the issues. I sought and asked for help, and subsequently resolved the problems facing me, with the aid of others. For most schools, their teachers' well-being is a top priority. Even as a supply teacher, I was vulnerable but I wasn't afraid to ask for help.

Unfortunately, the role did come to an end much sooner than expected. The following week, after working all day Monday and Tuesday, and having felt weak and poorly all day, I fell ill in the evening with viral symptoms. I left school at about 5.50pm on that final day. After a momentary chat, I wished both Hannah and Sally a good evening, and left them working at their desks. As I strolled up the long corridor towards the exit, I didn't know then that it would be my last day ever at the school.

This was at the beginning of the coronavirus pandemic, so with worsening symptoms, and in line with government advice, I had to self-isolate. The following day, the Prime Minister, Boris Johnson, announced that schools would close at the end of the week, although special arrangements were made for the children of key workers to continue to attend.

The headteacher subsequently informed the agency that my tenure had therefore come to an end, as a result of this announcement, and I learned later that a senior member of staff had been assigned to oversee the entire year group, including the class I had been teaching because a new kind of teaching would need to be quickly learned and implemented. It was called remote learning: a new method of teaching for nearly all educators at the time!

When I realised I would not be going back to the school, I texted my goodbyes to Hannah and Sally. In response, Sally kindly texted back and said, "…You have been a breath of fresh air – something none of us will be getting for a while." I recognised the pun in her comment, but also the kind compliment. Was I really a breath of fresh air? I found myself questioning if that had been true. Had I made a difference? On this occasion, I truly doubted myself, but I had to acknowledge that both colleagues, and particularly Hannah, who had only been a teacher for a year and a half, was an extremely competent leader, and capable beyond her years. Their positive opinions of me were certainly worth having, and I felt gratified that in spite of the stress and struggle I had faced in the job, I had not quit my assignment, even if I had come close at one point. The whole experience was a personal lesson in pressing forward, one small step at a time, even when the trials and challenges seem too much, and in choosing to be humble and teachable by accepting support and guidance from others.

A few months later, Sally kindly gathered the resources I had left behind in the classroom, which I had purchased out of my own pocket just for that class. I was then able to collect these items from her home, when it was safe to do so, as we were still in a pandemic. I once again shared with her that I had felt a hindrance to the team, and she repeated the phrase that I was a 'breath of fresh air' as we socially distanced at the doorstep.

Despite being a resilient supply teacher, there was one occasion though, when I did have to walk away from a teaching assignment, and I have never regretted that decision to this day. It occurred while I was working at a school for just a few days. The school, unfortunately, had a very negative reputation in the community, due to the behavioural problems of many of the children, and, according to my agency, struggled to attract supply teachers. My task was to cover a Year Six class on Wednesday, Thursday and Friday for just one week. As already shared, I have worked with some very challenging children in a variety of settings, but the behaviour I encountered in this class was one of the most drastic I have ever come across and is on a par with the two other classes I have already mentioned.

It was clear on my first day that this was no ordinary class, and at lunchtime, I expressed my concerns about the children's behaviour to the class teacher, Jenny. She was also part of the senior management team, so remained working in the school on the days I was covering. She had warned me that the children were, "A little noisy," but reassured me that I could address any problems with her.

The morning was horrendous! Despite following the school's behaviour policy and using all the class management strategies I knew, nothing worked. I had used discretion and tact. I had used a soft tone. I had used a firmer and louder voice. I had issued consequences. No matter what action was taken, most of the children just remained unresponsive. By lunchtime, there were a tumultuous number of concerns, which I needed to discuss with Jenny. I asked for a second adult to assist me, but Jenny said no one was available. The rest of the day continued in a similar vein.

Later that day, I rang my agency and spoke to one of the owners. She was very understanding and supportive and allowed me to make the decision of whether I would return to the school the next day. I slept on the dilemma I was in. Not wanting to quit, as is my usual attitude, I returned the following day determined to succeed, but it was another hard day, and I pleaded once more with Jenny for a supporting adult. I made it very clear I was really struggling with the class, but again, I was told there was no one free.

The final morning was a terrible struggle of 'uphill climbing' but getting nowhere. I made my request to Jenny yet again for support. I suppose I knew that my request was tenuous, but I asked anyway. The narrative was the same: there was no one to facilitate me, so basically just get on with it Mr Kersey! Even so, Jenny did offer to take the afternoon register in order to help settle the children. They were almost motionless during that registration, which didn't surprise me. This was, after all, their teacher.

Following the afternoon register, Jenny immediately left the classroom. I had to teach a personal, social, health and economic lesson (PSHE) for the afternoon, and needed to arrange the children into a large circle in the centre of the classroom. I quietly asked the children to help in moving the tables to the walls and

Lesson 4 - Vulnerability - Help!

setting up a circle of chairs in the centre. While the class were doing this, I noticed two boys were sitting at the back of the classroom wearing headphones. I gestured to them to join us. One removed his headphones and abruptly shouted, "What?" I warmly invited both boys to join us. He ignored me and placed his headphones back over his ears. They both continued to listen to music. A few of the children then explained to me that, as a reward, some children were allowed to listen to music during lesson time. How bizarre! I thought. Why had the teacher not made me aware of this reward?

Suddenly, I caught sight of a boy named Darren, standing on a table surface by an open window. One foot was on the table while another foot was resting on a radiator beneath the window. Upon seeing an ambulance arriving at the school, Darren leaned out the window and at the top of his voice shouted to the two paramedics, as they waited by the school office entrance. "You ******* idiots, we don't want you here!" This boy was one of the most indifferent pupils I have ever taught. While raising my voice at him, I rushed over to help him climb down, but he decided to bounce from one table to another. Eventually, I managed to coax him down. Almost immediately, three children decided to remove their shoes and dance on the tables in just their socks. Imagining all kinds of accidents just waiting to happen, I firmly told them to get down straight away. Fortunately, these three children did not need too much persuasion to carefully climb down from the tables and put their shoes back on. Without warning, an argument between some children behind me ensued, and tempers began to fray. A stool was tossed across the room, followed by a chair. I bellowed as loudly as I could and moved children out of the way. Two boys started a physical fight, while a girl threw a hardback book towards another girl's head. A few of the children were joining me in trying to stop the arguing and sporadic fighting.

Some of the children were completely feral and the situation was quickly escalating. I knew I needed help. I felt I had been climbing up a steep mountain, with crumbling terrain beneath my feet, burdened with an onerous load on my shoulders, and no offer of a lifeline for support. I opened the classroom door and left it wide open, knowing that Jenny was sat at a computer just several metres away in the corridor. It seemed that she had just ignored the loud noise and commotion up to this point.

Within seconds of my opening the classroom door, and as I expected, she burst into the room and shouted, "What on earth is going on here? Sit down the lot of you!" The class meekly followed her instruction and sat down. The classroom was in disarray.

I then said, with a calm but firm voice, "Thank you to those who have been sensible, but the behaviour of most of you over the past three days, has been diabolical and probably the worst I have ever seen. Some of you really need to think about your actions."

With this, Jenny looked at me and said, "Mr Kersey, I think you need to calm down. Perhaps go and have a cup of tea in the staff room." I was mortified! Her dictatorial tone startled me. It was unbelievable and inexplicable. How dare a fellow professional speak to me in such a disrespectful way in front of the children! For the past three days, she had seemed oblivious to my disquiet. No attempts to try and find a solution, other than taking the Friday afternoon register for me, had been forthcoming from her. She knew full well how disruptive her class was. If there was no support, then perhaps she should have chosen the most appropriate course of action and taught the class herself. A drastic decision I know, but we are talking about three days of constant safeguarding concerns being raised by me.

Such was my disgust with her, that I said not a word to her and acquiesced with her mentality. There was no point protesting, particularly in front of the children. Some educators just don't know how to listen! Instead, I silently collected my bag and my jacket and headed towards the headteacher's office.

Unfortunately, I discovered that neither the headteacher, nor the deputy head, were in school that day. I made my way to the front office, but again no one was there. Fortunately, a concerned colleague, who was also on the senior leadership team, had witnessed the outrageous behaviour going on in the classroom that afternoon as she walked past. She listened to me and confirmed my thoughts that I should have been given adult support for that class. She then told me that I had been allocated the most difficult class in the entire school. I expressed my disappointment with the class conduct, and also with Jenny, who had completely failed to take my concerns seriously. I made it clear that I would not be teaching the class for the remainder of the afternoon due to safeguarding concerns.

We returned to the class, and she notified Jenny that I would not be returning. Again, I said not a word. I was so disappointed by Jenny's treatment of me, not just then but over the three days, that I chose not to waste my breath further.

I left the school and immediately rang my agency to report the matter to them. Again, I spoke to one of the owners, who assured me she would personally call the school to express her dissatisfaction with the way I had been treated. She said she would also make it clear that since I, as their strongest teacher, had been treated so poorly, they would not be sending any further supply teachers from the agency.

Perhaps if Jenny had listened to me on the first day, and then acted upon my advice, the situation might not have escalated the way it did, or it could have been averted altogether. Jenny's insouciance was certainly frustrating and regretful. Being a team player works both ways of course, and it is very debilitating and discouraging for any educator, but particularly a visiting adult, when they notice something wrong or concerning which needs addressing but are ignored time and again when they report it.

The children's behaviour in this class was clearly shocking! Yet, while I am no expert in child psychology, I believe that children in general want to do the right thing. They want to please! The reasons why some children make wrong choices varies. For a start, their brains are still developing. The failure to put in place clear parameters especially at home, and a lack of good role models, are two other factors. How a child is treated and spoken to at home can affect their emotional and psychological growth, and they need adults around them to firmly correct them with love when they do wrong and encourage and praise them when they make any positive effort.

Nevertheless, every so often I encounter a child who appears to have no desire to do good, and they can make me feel very unsettled and uncomfortable. I have already shared one example of such a child. Perhaps it is their extremely aggressive and abhorrent behaviour, or their constant manipulation of situations to achieve their own ends. It might be because of the catatonic state they enter when I try to reason with them, their lack of remorse for any wrongdoing or their ability to fool professionals. It might be because of all these factors combined. Of course, all these children have a story to tell, and experience tells me that their bad behaviour often stems from some pain and trauma they have experienced, and perhaps continue to experience. Darren, the boy who swore at the paramedics, was just such a child. He was aggressive, disruptive, selfish, heartless and unconcerned with making good choices. In the short time I knew him, he resisted any attempts I made to engage with him, or to face consequences for his actions, and he showed no affection or care for his classmates. Fortunately, such children are rare, but I sense their potential to cause harm in later life if they continued on the path they have begun, spiralling further and further down. I am certain that such children need clear boundaries explained and set, accountability, responsibility for their own actions, and consequences for deliberate and intentional wrong choices. Equally, they also need extensive professional help, guidance, support, nurturing and monitoring, and above all, an abundance of love and compassion.

At the end of the day, like any educator, I am not superhuman, although some children will look at me with wide, starry eyes in adoration, as though I am. Nonetheless, I believe that in order to be successful, I need to know my limitations so that I can develop them into strengths over time. Each of us knows best how we cope when faced with personal conflicts and challenges. Yet the mental health and well-being of staff needs to be a top priority for all schools because the pressures teachers face is colossal. High expectations from some parents, appalling behaviour from some children, and the constant bombardment of extra work from some leadership, have all been contributing factors towards the mental health issues of some educators. For some educators it is literally about getting through the morning and then the afternoon – mentally surviving from one day to the next! For them, the weekend cannot ever come quick enough! Thankfully, talking about personal concerns, anxieties and fears is now encouraged in our society, but it still remains easy to make assumptions about others. Many suffer in silence and can be easily overlooked. These silent sufferers are both children and adults.

I never returned to that school where I worked for those three days. It became a 'poisoned chalice' and one of the very few schools on the south coast that I refused to ever work at again. Some days in class are swallowed up dealing with child and classroom issues, rather than actual constructive teaching, and what happened at that school was a prime example of this. When the childrens' behaviour is so extreme, so violent and continuous, and no colleague seems to be listening to my growing concerns, or colleagues have become so disrespectful and detestable towards me, or have spread half-truths and lies about me, then my wellbeing must be the priority. I have learnt in life that to preserve my mental health, I just need to turn around and quietly walk away from such toxic people and situations. Respectfully defending myself with such adults just adds 'flames to their fuel' from my experience. They become their own worst enemy by the way they speak to and treat others, and there is a sense of freedom, peace and satisfaction from walking away from toxic environments - leaving them behind forever. I have 'burnt several bridges' over the years and have no regrets in doing so. A 'poisoned pathway' is too risky to return to. The pain can be greater though when it is management that you expected to trust.

Lesson 5

Trust

Don't Stop Believin'

Trust, in my opinion, is probably the most fundamental 'lesson' in my book. How can any individual or business thrive and succeed without it? Eventually, they will be caught out if there is not that element of trust, particularly if they are in positions of management and leadership. When management has let me down, I try to maintain self-belief. Life is certainly tough for all of us at times, but we must keep going, keep persevering, moving forward, and believing in ourselves and others. Walking away from an extreme challenge, as was shared in the previous chapter, does not mean that I had taken a step backwards. On the contrary, I needed to adjust and correct my course, and then continue on my upward trajectory with my career.

There is a wise quote from the Scottish author, poet and Christian minister, George MacDonald, who said, "To be trusted is a greater compliment than being loved."[9]

When a colleague at work trusts me, it is an honour and a reflection of my reputation and character. Trust should be the primary trait of anyone who has a duty of care with children. It should

Lesson 5 - Trust - Don't Stop Believin'

also exist with those who are in a position of authority. The majority of headteachers that I have met, seemed to have shown care and trust towards their staff. I think of several headteachers and deputy heads who I have worked with who stand out to me. Each have influenced, encouraged and looked for the positives in those they are responsible for. They have led by example! Disappointedly, I have seen a few headteachers and deputy heads, who have abused their position of trust, and caused great mental suffering on others. I often wonder why such individuals were appointed in the first place. A leader should inspire, build and motivate through their own example and words. It is not just in education that I have seen some examples of both good and poor leadership in place. Having worked in various sectors over the decades, I have seen dreadful management in other working environments too.

By far the worse example of a leader abusing their position of authority, that I have been directly affected by, was not in an education setting at all, but while I was serving as a new recruit in the Metropolitan Police Service.

I recall my early years as a police constable in London, and the initial training at Hendon Police School. Despite its very demanding schedule and high expectations, the training at Hendon was a real joy of learning and personal growth for me. The tutors were superb, and there was great camaraderie among everyone in the class. Life couldn't have been better for me!

It was towards the end of this five-month training, that myself and four other recruits were informed that we would be continuing our training on division together. The next day, one of these recruits, a female in her early 40s named PC Carrie, worryingly told us that she had shared this news with her partner, who was a serving police officer at another division. He responded by telling her that Sgt Tanning worked at the division where we were going to be sent. He told her that this particular man was nasty and had a fearsome reputation of getting rid of new recruits. This news didn't exactly fill us with confidence! Surely, this man couldn't be as bad as that?

We would very soon realise how cruel this man really was. His reputation had spread to other parts of the Met like an out of control wildfire. No one, it seemed, had extinguished his insatiable appetite for crushing what little confidence and enthusiasm a new recruit may have had.

The contrast in the environment at Hendon Police School to what I experienced, in particular in the first few months after being deployed on division, couldn't have been more obvious. If 'Hell' existed in the workplace, then it did during that period of time for me, and I know for my fellow new recruits too. Some of the instructors were extremely unpleasant, but notably the group leader named Sergeant (Sgt) Tanning: a single male in his 40s and a seasoned police officer. Bullying and intimidation was rife, and he seemed intent on inflicting great stress and extreme mental pressure on us all.

There were 'initiations' we had to endure, such as cleaning

the canteen fridge in front of other officers who were eating. While on our hands and knees cleaning the fridge, some officers would peel citrus fruit, split them so the juices were starting to seep out, then aim them at the back of our heads. I recall cleaning the fridge one day and seeing an orange projectile come flying across the room from the corner of my eye. In a split second, the orange had hit the neck of one of my fellow recruits named PC Phillips, who was kneeling down while cleaning the fridge with me. Sticky orange juice trickled down the back of his neck and white shirt as officers laughed at his misfortune.

On another occasion, we were all required to clean a couple of police carriages (large vans). These carriages were normally reserved for riots and demonstrations, and they resembled white tanks. They were huge! It was November, the weather was cold, and the carriages were filthy. We were given buckets to fill with cold water and soap suds, and told to scrub the carriages - with only toothbrushes! I recall it taking us nearly half the shift to complete the job. I had no problem with tough, physical grafting - I once worked as a builder's labourer for about eighteen months. That was incredibly hard, physical work, especially in the bitterly cold months. A builder's labourer is certainly not a job for wimps, and I did that job efficiently and without complaint. In my opinion though, the ridiculous task of washing large police vans with toothbrushes was not a productive use of police time. It was probably an opportunity for Sgt Tanning and a few others to be amused at our expense.

Lesson 5 - Trust - Don't Stop Believin'

The humiliation and degradation continued each day for us new recruits. Then several weeks later, we were all taken to a busy part of town with shops, cafes and restaurants. Sgt Tanning told us collectively not to return to the police station until we had each issued twenty parking tickets. As there were five of us, that would total one hundred parking fines in an 8-hour shift – on Christmas Eve! We were about as popular with the public as someone breaking wind in a crowded lift! Many of the local community despised us as they wished us a 'Happy Christmas!'

Nearing the end of my shift, a man asked me if he could park his car on double yellow lines while he nipped into the chemist. Having some compassion on him, I said I'd allow him a few minutes. However, I was in a conundrum and panicked when I realised that I needed several more tickets written out, or Sgt Tanning would be very displeased with me, and there could be repercussions for failing him. Such was the pressure on me, that I issued a ticket after a minute or two. I didn't see the driver after issuing the ticket, but he drove straight to the Divisional Headquarters to see the Chief Superintendent to complain. Shortly afterwards, I was called into his office to be given a right verbal scolding. Little did the Chief Superintendent know the truth about the ridiculous and unfair targets we had each been set that Christmas Eve day. We were just Sgt Tanning's pawns!

I am convinced that Sgt Tanning wanted new recruits to quit the Force, but we all knew better. Personally, I had joined the Met to serve and protect the public. A standard comment I know, but

I believed in myself and knew the qualities I possessed would contribute to the positive image of the police at the time. It is ironic that someone who was meant to uphold the law, was simultaneously abusing his position of authority.

I was different in Sgt Tanning's eyes, and therefore it appeared obvious that I was his, and a few of the instructors, number one target. They seemed to have a hang up with the fact that I wasn't verbally or physically aggressive towards members of the public. Upon seeing this treatment towards me, PC Carrie, who had previously been employed by Amnesty International, said to me one day, "Grant, what you are experiencing is religious persecution. I saw it in my previous job at Amnesty International." Whatever their reasons for being so vindictive, for me personally, I just wanted to uphold good values in my new profession - just like the majority of my police colleagues, including the other new recruits.

Sgt Tanning bluntly asked me one day, "Why can't you be like everyone else?" What's wrong with being unique? Were we born to be robots, having no thoughts of our own? I was very willing to be like all the 'good cops' but I had zero interest in following a small number of instructors, who I deemed as cruel and objectionable in their conduct. Their strange attitudes were made clear one evening, when one of the instructors, an experienced constable, saw me opening the front nearside door of a vehicle I had stopped for having a faulty front light. After speaking to the driver about his light, carrying out a name and vehicle check, which came back all clear, and then giving him a written warning to fix the light within seven days, I noticed the passenger door was ajar. Standing on the pavement, I bent down, knocked on the window and indicated to the driver, as he was to drive off, that the door was still open. I opened the door and slammed it shut for him. He put his thumbs up, smiled, and drove off. I thought nothing of this act, but my instructor, who was accompanying a few of us recruits that evening, was absolutely incensed. "What the bloody hell are you doing 403?" he screamed. (We were never called by our names). I calmly gave the reason for closing the front passenger door, to which he replied, "You know what your problem is 403? You're too nice!" Well, if that was my only crime, then yes, I was guilty as charged, I thought to myself.

A few days later, one of my fellow recruits named PC Keegan, overheard these instructors talking about me. They were discussing how to 'toughen me up.' PC Keegan then cautiously interjected, and said to them, "I hope you don't mind me interrupting your conversation, but Grant was asked to box for Hendon. I've seen him box. He can look after himself."

As part of our training at Hendon, each recruit had been put in a boxing ring with another recruit of similar weight. They were then told to beat each other for a whole minute. The PE instructors wanted to see if we could give a punch and take a punch. However, they had placed me in the ring with two men, who I nearly knocked out. Afterwards, one of the PE instructors, who had a flattened nose like a hardened bouncer, approached me and said, "Have you boxed before? You are a natural boxer! Would you be interested in boxing for Hendon at the Met Police Boxing Tournament?" I hadn't had any previous training or experience of boxing, other than a few school fights with bullies in high school, but I was pleased to receive the recognition. I participated in some boxing training at Hendon Police School after that, in preparation for the tournament. However, some weeks later I received the news that the tournament, for reasons unbeknown to me, had been cancelled that year. I was hugely disappointed upon hearing this, and never got the chance to show my boxing skills in a ring again.

In response to PC Keegan's comment to the group, the acting sergeant replied, "So why can't he be aggressive with the public?" What a moronic mindset! We were being mentored by a bunch of instructors, whom some considered it a sign of strength to be rude and physically aggressive to the public, when it wasn't necessary. Yes, if I had been faced with a violent individual, then I would have had no hesitation in taking them down and detaining that person, but that situation hadn't presented itself to me, thus far in my police training.

Many times, and not just during my service while on-duty, but prior to joining the Met Police, while off-duty during my police service, and ever since, I have had to intervene to pacify agitated individuals, stop potential fights, street robberies, assaults, wanton acts of criminal damage, and even thwart burglars. My family know that I have never shied away from calming down a situation, preventing a criminal act being carried out, or even apprehending an offender until police have arrived.

One of numerous examples of this was just six years ago, in the autumn of 2017, when I disturbed two burglars who had broken into my neighbour's bungalow. Upon hearing the breaking of glass from the rear of their property, I was over the garden wall, dialling 999, and straight into the home within a minute or so.

During the scuffle, one of the burglars lost his trainer and dropped a package of drugs wrapped in clingfilm. Both the fingerprints from the package and the prints from the trainer sole, placed these two at the crime scene of many burglaries in the area. Both individuals were identified and subsequently tracked down months later. They had literally terrorised the neighbourhood – until they met me on that dark and drizzly night!

My neighbour's home, according to police, was the only home in the area where no property had been stolen. The burglars had left a pillowcase with stashed jewellery and other valuables in one of the bedrooms, and an open wallet full of cash on the bed. They were very quick, but such had been my swift entrance, and probably much to their shock as well, that they fled empty handed that evening.

My reward, other than the personal satisfaction that nothing had been stolen from my retired neighbour's property, was a delicious steak meal treat a couple of months later – all paid for by my very grateful neighbours.

In 1996, I received a Superintendent's Commendation for effecting the arrest of three burglars – on two separate occasions – whilst off duty! You could say that catching burglars is in my blood!

Lesson 5 - Trust - Don't Stop Believin'

Therefore, for Sgt Tanning and a few of his mates to assume that I was somehow afraid to get involved in precarious situations or deal with violent individuals, was actually an insult to me. They got me so wrong!

Upon hearing about the off-duty arrests, through a colleague of mine - namely my Relief Inspector, the Divisional Commander at my division wrote to me in August of 1994, stating that, "The Metropolitan Police Service has burglary, high on the list of priorities and you have shown courage and tenacity in contributing to our success." She then stated in the letter that she would be recommending me for a Deputy Assistant Commissioner's (DAC) Commendation. To accept this award, I had to sign a form and return both the form and her letter, to her, which I promptly did via the internal dispatch.

About a year and a half went by and I had received no further response from her office. So, I decided to follow up on her recommendation. I was told by Admin at the divisional station, that no such letter from the Divisional Commander could be found. It seemed the letter from her had mysteriously or perhaps 'conveniently' disappeared.

However, I was one step ahead, and had photocopied the original letter before placing it, and the signed form, in dispatch, which I duly presented to her office.

With this evidence, the Divisional Commander agreed that I should indeed be awarded a commendation. However, as the rank of DAC was no longer in use by this time, it was decided by the

Lesson 5 - Trust - Don't Stop Believin'

powers that be, that I should be given the honoured, but much lesser regarded, Superintendent's Commendation instead.

Oh well – but at least I did receive a commendation of some kind, even if it wasn't the more distinguished Deputy Assistant Commissioner's Commendation as originally suggested.

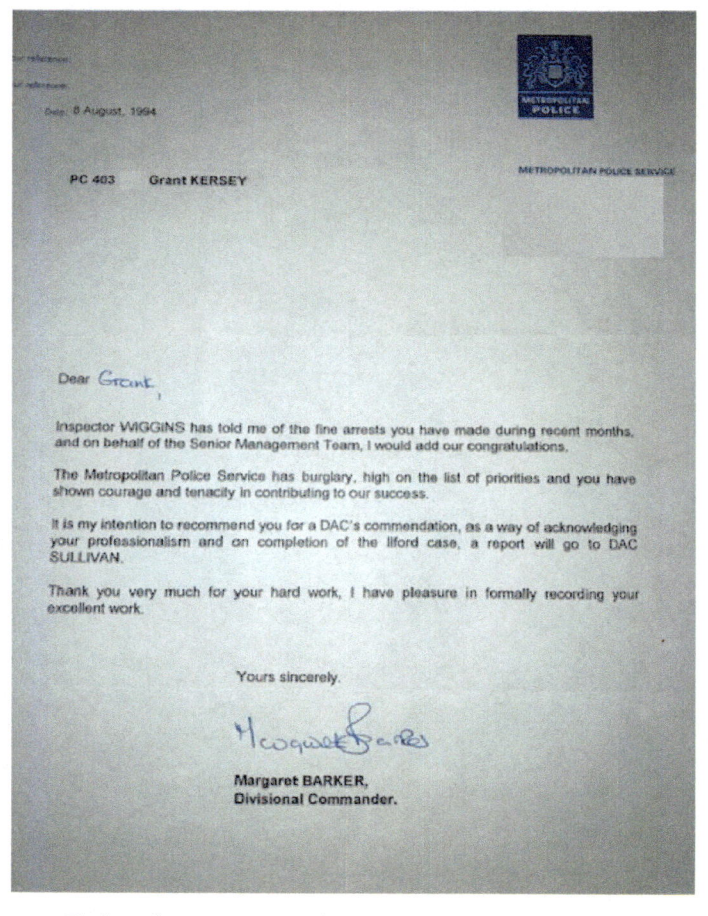

The letter from my Divisional Commander, recommending me for a Deputy Assistant Commissioner's Commendation

Lesson 5 - Trust - Don't Stop Believin'

July 1996 – me and my wife after receiving my Superintendent's Commendation for bravery

As time went by, I despised a few of these instructors, who frequently behaved like intimidating and uncouth thugs. Perhaps they viewed themselves as 'top dogs' at the station, but they were more crass than badass. Some of the instructors considered the principles of upright behaviour as a weakness, yet their mindset couldn't have been further from the truth. It takes tremendous self-discipline, great courage and mental strength to be dignified, calm and respectful, particularly towards those who despise and openly mock you.

On another occasion, Sgt Tanning said he wanted a 'word' with me in the Custody Suite at one of the stations. This Custody Suite had not been used for years, and no one really had the need to go in there. With one of his sidekicks sitting on a bench behind him, he quietly said to me, "Do you know what the term 'battery' means?" "Yes. Why?" I replied. "Well take this!" he whispered. With that, he punched me firmly in the chest, took one step backwards, then remained staring at me with his fists raised high. His punch didn't shake me physically and I stood my ground. I was dealing with an idiot! However, I could have easily returned fire and hit him squarely in the face, and I knew that if I did, I would have sent him flying. Nevertheless, with his pal acting as his witness, that would not have been a good move for me. I knew if I physically retaliated, I would be out of a job. I said not a word to him, turned around and silently walked away.

Reflecting upon that incident, I wished I had reported that assault on me because there was considerable justification to do so

– even if no one believed me, it would have been worth it.

Like my new colleagues, we all took the harsh mistreatment 'on the chin' so to speak, and we tried to keep our heads down and out of trouble. For me, my inner emotions were always channelled, with a hope for better days ahead giving me something to cling to. I kept that belief in myself always at the back of mind.

It was during this very 'dark' and traumatic time in my life, which felt more like a prison sentence, that an illuminating light entered my life in the form of my future wife. I finally had someone outside of work, who I could talk to about the treatment the new recruits and I were being subjected to. Unsurprisingly, she was very shocked and concerned, and became a pillar of strength and a source of great moral support and reassurance to me.

When us new recruits were eventually placed with a relief, Sgt Tanning, fortunately, was not on the same team as me.

About a year or so later, during a training session at another police station, the five of us new recruits opened up to a senior police officer. We were finally able to collectively report Sgt Tanning's terrible treatment and bullying. Consequently, Sgt Tanning was immediately stopped from ever training recruits fresh out of Hendon Police School.

Nonetheless, he and his inner circle of a few colleagues, hounded me for a few years afterwards, and consequently, I struggled with confidence during the early years of my police career. Those initial few months under Sgt Tanning's 'tutelage' was so traumatic for me, that it had a knock-on effect with my ability to focus on duty thereafter.

I would arrive at the police station for duty, and immediately check the radio log or duty roster to see if Sgt Tanning was also on duty. It was not unusual for there to be more than one relief on duty on the same day. Overlapping of shifts by different teams was common. For example, one relief might be assigned the 8am to 4pm shift, while another relief might be working 2pm to 10pm. If I could see that Sgt Tanning was on duty, then great anxiety would come over me. If I discovered that he was based at the divisional station as the Custody Sgt, then I tried to avoid arresting anyone, purely so that I wouldn't have to face him. It was the first time I had ever experienced stress and great anxiety in the workplace, and it was solely because of him and a few men who supported him.

One day, I had been invited by my relief to join them at the Old Bailey (the central criminal court of England and Wales in Central London) to attend the sentencing of a convicted murderer, who had stabbed to death one of our sergeants a year or two earlier. The next day, I heard that Sgt Tanning had actively been searching for me on the day of sentencing. He had assumed that I had not been invited to the sentencing, and so he wanted to find me – no doubt to incessantly harass me once again.

Redemption, to a certain degree, came a few years later, when Sgt Tanning's tight group individually seemed to accept me. I suppose that came as a result of them and others getting to know the real me, and my good work ethic. As for Sgt Tanning himself, it took the day of his retirement several years later, before he finally called me by my first name for the very first time. Before that, I was just a number to him. I had approached him at his and another colleague's retirement social gathering, and extended my hand. As I shook his hand, and looked him directly in the eye, I said, "All the best (first name withheld)." To my surprise, he replied, "You too Grant!" This ruthless man was wishing me all the best! Did he really have a soft side to his nature?

It is difficult to describe the inner joy that that moment brought to me. Hearing him calling me by my first name was a defining moment for me, and I finally felt accepted by him. It is such a shame however, that that 'welcoming attitude' hadn't been offered to me years earlier.

Sadly, Sgt Tanning, is to this day, the nastiest person I have ever had the misfortune of working with and under. I am aware that two of those new recruits, whom I am still in contact with, still bare a great dislike for him. He was in a position of authority, and should have shown us care, positive guidance and support. Instead, he chose to be a prolific bully with a dreadful reputation.

Over thirty years later, I still have the occasional dream where I am on duty and thrown in the 'lion's den' with Sgt Tanning and his mates. They are hounding me, mocking me and making my life a living hell. The emotional feeling is always the same: I am sick to the stomach with worry and anxiety. I just want to run away – but there is no choice except to stay!

That was spiteful and vindictive leadership at its extreme, and the workplace bullying I suffered was totally superfluous and outdated. It should have been resigned to a bygone era. The severe treatment was excessively disproportionate to what the average member of the public, or indeed, a normal minded, serving police officer, would expect a new police recruit to have to endure.

However, despite the hate, harassment and workplace bullying at its worst, Sgt Tanning couldn't break my resolve to do what I felt was morally right, rather than appeasing him and his improprieties. That experience helped mould my character further, and taught me greater patience, tolerance and resilience when faced with obnoxious and manipulative individuals, especially at work.

When leaders and managers treat any of their staff with rudeness, intimidation, bullying or aggressive behaviour, including passive aggressive conduct, they lose the trust of those they have responsibility for, and consequently, they deter their staff from producing the best possible results. Victims of workplace bullying can become physically and mentally ill and may end up going on sick leave. In more extreme cases, they may even take their own lives. From my observations, the most productive and impactful schools have leadership which genuinely cares and treats all staff with respect. The management style is one of support rather than exploitation. Thus, they get the best out of their staff because the staff feel appreciated and are settled and happy to work there.

Leadership in schools will have good intentions but occasionally those good intentions, blinded by a lack of vision or understanding, actually create more problems than solutions. Of all the bodies of power that influence education, it has to be government which often fails to deliver. Ministers and the Office for Standards in Education, Children's Services and Skills (Ofsted) will seemingly be the most publicly vocal to criticise schools and educators, rather than encourage. They can also be the last to heap any praise too.

A perfect example of this has to be the comments made in January 2021 by the then education secretary, Gavin Williamson, when he disappointedly encouraged parents to complain to Ofsted if their child's school was not providing satisfactory remote learning. Mr Williamson could have chosen a different tactic and shown his understanding of the unique pressures that educators were facing, by expressing his appreciation for their tireless efforts. As is typical with out of touch leadership, detached from the realities faced at grassroots level, he chose to focus on the negatives by wanting to show educators in a poor light. He wanted to embarrass schools! Quoting from the Guardian, he said, "We expect schools to provide between three and five hours teaching a day, depending on the child's age. If parents feel their child's school is not providing suitable remote education they should first raise their concerns with the teacher or headteacher and, failing that, report the matter to Ofsted."[10]

This ill-informed and thoughtless statement from Mr Williamson, was insulting to hardworking educators, and a 'smack in the face' for struggling teachers still trying to learn and adapt to teaching remotely, and subsequently deal with the myriad of related issues and difficulties. It was indicative of a minister out of touch with educators, and indeed many parents it seemed. For most people, including educators, I'm sure that the word 'Zoom' as a software platform for teaching remotely, was unheard of prior to the pandemic.

Covid-19 had presented schools with unprecedented challenges, and extra financial burdens on schools too, due to having to purchase extra resources such as more wash basins, soaps, masks, hand sanitisers, drinking fountains and so on.

Can you just imagine the uproar if the Health Secretary at the time had made a public statement which encouraged the public to complain about the National Health Service (NHS) if staff and hospital management were not performing their duties efficiently because of delays in non-emergency procedures, lack of beds and increased waiting lists?

Not surprisingly, Mr Williamson's comments backfired, and Ofsted was inundated with emails from parents who praised schools for their efforts at the time. However, the thousands of positive emails from parents clogged up Ofsted's website and delayed the time to find emails related to actual safeguarding matters and other important business. The timing by a government minister was once again completely wrong.

Trust between management and ground level staff is of course a 'two-way street' and runs through the 'veins' of a safe and successful school. Therefore, there is no argument that being trustworthy is of the very highest priority. It is paramount in every aspect of my professional life, and the welfare and safety of the children in my care is of the greatest consideration, as it is for all educators.

Nonetheless, as a guest in the schools for which I provide cover, there is another way in which I am expected to be trustworthy. This includes respecting and taking care of the classroom resources and equipment, and any personal property I might come across in the course of my work. Although I am effectively autonomous, I also represent my agency. In addition, I must abide by each school's guidelines and policies, as previously discussed. It is imperative that I can be trusted because it is fundamental to being a successful supply teacher.

For example, when I finish my assignment at the end of the day, I try to leave the classroom either in the state it was found, which was hopefully tidy, or in the way I would want to find it if I were the full-time teacher.

During my time as a full-time teacher, I found it very frustrating when my classroom was left in a mess by a TA, HLTA, specialist teacher or supply teacher. It was exasperating to arrive early in the morning and find my classroom cluttered, with books from the book corner lying in a heap, tables pushed out of position, and worksheets, scrap paper, pens, rulers, rubbers and highlighter pens scattered on the tables and floor. Sometimes, even my own desk was strewn with all manner of debris. On such occasions, it was frustrating to have to take precious time first thing in the morning to tidy the entire classroom. I consider it selfish not to leave any classroom I have used in good order. If there is not time for the children to tidy up at the end of the day, then it is my responsibility to take care of the tidying up, after the children have been collected.

I recall, while I was working under contract as a long-term supply teacher, that the decision to use my classroom was imposed upon me. However, at the end of the Inset day, I was left to clear up alone. Tables were out of their proper positions, and there were papers, pens, personal iPads, and other electronic devices lying abandoned on the tables. There was even a colleague's memory stick in my laptop! I had no idea whose it was as there had been a handful of educators giving presentations. Thankfully, one thoughtful teacher returned to help me tidy. A little consideration goes a long way!

On a visit to a school in Hampshire in early 2019, I sat to the side of the classroom while the full-time teacher announced to the children that I would be teaching them for the afternoon. As they were tidying up in readiness for lunchbreak, she asked, "Now make sure you tidy up our classroom, just like Mr Kersey always expects you to." Looking over to me, she smiled and announced, "He always leaves this classroom so neat and tidy, and we are very grateful to him." That was clearly a thoughtful gesture from a teacher, who acknowledged and openly praised my efforts to keep her classroom well-kept, whenever I would teach her class. For anyone using a colleague's classroom, I think the message is very clear and doesn't need to be spelled out further.

Likewise, all teachers, in my experience, appreciate my feedback. If there is no opportunity to speak to the teacher whether face-to-face or via email or to the class supporting adult for them to pass on to the teacher, I try to take the time to leave written feedback, and ensure it is left in a prominent place. This may sound an obvious and expected task, but I am surprised how many teachers thank me for my written feedback, and mention that some supply teachers don't make the effort to leave any. Upon their return, the teacher will surely want to know about the children's progress and behaviour during their absence. They will be keen to know who received any class/school rewards, who misbehaved, who received a 'bump note' following an accident, any conflicts that needed dealing with, who completed work independently or who required support. If I support a small group of children with any of their lessons, or if I am unable to teach the entire lesson plan left for me, I make a note of these details on sticky notes. After school, I can refer to these notes when I write my feedback. I might mention any child taken home early due to illness or colleagues who have assisted me, as well as any verbal messages left by parents. Finally, I always express my appreciation for the plans, daily schedule and worksheets left for me by the teacher. This detailed feedback acts as a 'diary entry' and informs the absent teacher on their return.

I also take seriously the trust placed in me to mark all the work the children do while I am teaching them, using the school's marking policy. I know this eases the pressure for the regular teacher when they return, and that leaving a pile of books for them to mark is unhelpful. I consider this an important responsibility. Indeed, my reputation is at stake! Teaching is a small world, and if I am careless or lazy, other professionals will soon find out as word spreads. I genuinely take pride in my work, and take time to show that I care. I like to think that I treat others, and their property, in the way I would like to be treated.

I have witnessed on countless occasions, the positive effect that trust between parents and the school can have on a child's education and development. It is key, but not necessarily a guarantee, to a child's educational and future career opportunities and successes. As the parent of three children myself, I know the pivotal role my wife and I had to play in our children's educational development and well-being. In my experience, the vast majority of parents are respectful to the educators, loving to their child, and supportive of their child's learning.

I was touched by one example of parents who gave total support to their wayward child, while teaching at a school in Bournemouth. They were separated, and were initially in competition with each other, rather than supporting their son, named Dan.

Dan had received a great deal of support, especially from his teachers, and his one-to-one adult, Kath, since his arrival at the school, but progress was painfully slow. The conflict at home had been a major hurdle for Dan, and had also created problems for those involved in his education when they tried to reach out to the parents.

Then one year, Dan's behaviour began to change. When I taught his class again, about a year later in 2019, I was amazed by how much progress Dan had made since our paths had last crossed. He was no longer selfish, argumentative and attention-seeking, but rather considerate, respectful, inclined to give rather than take, and keenly engaged with all his learning. I was delighted by the change, and commented on it to Kath. "What has made the difference?" I enquired. She enthusiastically told me that although his parents remained separated, they had agreed to put aside their differences so that they could give Dan, and his educational needs, top priority in their lives. They worked together, and with the school. They listened and acted. It worked! This change in attitude and behaviour on the part of his parents was pivotal in turning Dan around. It had a ripple effect on him. Now that his parents and the school were working as a unit to help him, Dan was able to thrive. To have children's parents working with the school, and 'singing from the same song sheet' is vital for them to achieve their full potential.

On the other hand, I believe one of the greatest challenges facing modern teachers is a lack of respect from a small number of parents. As stated, the majority of parents are gracious and supportive but a minority of challenging parents, as well as children, can cause a colossal amount of time-consuming extra meetings, emails, form filling, reports, assessments and stress for the educators.

Sometimes, those children who are disrespectful to teachers

are allowed to be disrespectful at home, and their parents may not have applied rules and boundaries or imposed any kind of discipline. I do not, of course, endorse physical punishment of any kind. However, parents need to impose sanctions for bad behaviour, and follow through with them with conditions. Children must know there are consequences for wrongdoing. When children come from chaotic homes, where these basic parenting rules are not followed, their parents all too often expect, and even demand, that their wayward child's teacher should affect some kind of miracle remedy.

Yet, it is parents who first set the tone for their child's day at school. Screaming and swearing at a child in the morning before school, will likely set a negative tone for their day ahead. I have seen children entering class so upset from an incident at home that morning, that they then find it very difficult to erase the hurtful comments or inappropriate behaviour they have just witnessed. They can find it hard to focus on the learning and struggle to concentrate. It is no surprise then when that child has a bad day at school.

I have of course been charged with communicating with parents on so many occasions. I always listen to those parents, take mental or even written notes, if needed, and pass on information to other educators where necessary. Furthermore, I implement any suggestions, where appropriate, and follow up on parental concerns and requests. I have had a very healthy relationship with parents over the years.

From time to time, but fortunately not too often, I have been

Lesson 5 - Trust - Don't Stop Believin'

confronted by very agitated parents. I remain calm and respectful and try not to take any criticisms personally. They love their child and want whatever is causing them any angst to be resolved.

An example of this occurred when I was covering for two terms at one of my favourite schools, in mid-Dorset. After my first week there, I was informed that a mother, named Mrs Keeling, wanted to speak with me about her son, Frankie, who was in my class. I was advised not to meet alone with Mrs Keeling, and so one of the TAs, named Sharna, agreed to stay after school so that we could meet with Frankie and his mother together.

At the meeting, which was actually on the playground because Mrs Keeling did not wish to enter the school building, I warmly introduced myself to her. She immediately launched into a tirade of abuse, making it very clear she felt that the headteacher and other members of staff showed no concern for Frankie's welfare. She cited past incidents when a classmate, named Steven, had bullied Frankie, asserting angrily that no action had been taken. "Nothing has been done about it!" She angrily bellowed. Mrs Keeling then mentioned another bullying incident that had taken place that day involving Steven. I confirmed with Frankie why he had not told anyone in school what had happened and reminded him of the importance of speaking to an adult immediately when such incidents occur, rather than waiting to tell his mum after school. Mrs Keeling then threatened to assault Steven physically by slapping his face and drop kicking him if she were to see him.

I then looked her in the eye, and said, "You will not threaten a child on these premises, nor will you harm a child. Do you understand Mrs Keeling?" She changed her tone a little after this but began to encourage Frankie to assault Steven instead. He was staring at his mother, looking somewhat dazed, nodding at her instructions. I gently, but firmly, called his name, and when he looked at me, I said, "Frankie, you must not hit other children, or harm them in any way. Do you understand?" He looked first at me, then at his mother, who continued to goad him with fighting talk. Frankie was confused and hesitant, and I spoke to him again, "Don't listen to what your mum is asking you to do, Frankie. It's wrong!" He hesitated, but I prompted him to look at me, and he fixed his eyes on me again, and nodded in agreement.

Not wanting the meeting to end so abruptly and on a sour note, I placated Mrs Keeling by reassuring her that she could speak with me at any time. I told her I would always be more than happy to listen to her, and I promised that I would follow up on any concerns she might have. I wished Frankie and his mum a good weekend as they departed.

Sharna and I discussed the meeting briefly, and then I reported it to the headteacher, Mr Carson, who immediately implemented measures both to safeguard Steven, and to meet Frankie's needs.

My approach may have seemed unconventional to some, but nevertheless, it worked. I could see she was openly exhibiting her frustrations because of what she perceived as bullying by another boy towards her son, and also what she felt was a lack of care from the school, and I felt a little sorry for her. Despite having had to verbally reprimand her, I wanted to help her feel some trust towards me.

Over the months that followed, Mrs Keeling continued to refuse to enter the school premises because of her dislike for all the staff, but she often met with me at the school gate to discuss Frankie and her concerns about him. Over time, her attitude softened, and she learned to trust me. I always followed up on anything she was worried about, and reported Frankie's progress promptly, which she appreciated.

We discovered that we shared a passion for football, but while she supported Millwall, I was a West Ham United fan. The rivalry between the two clubs goes back more than a hundred years, when Millwall supporters were generally dockers in South-East London, while the Hammers worked in the nearby iron factories in East London. Although they were neighbours, they were, and continue to be, bitter rivals. The irony was not lost on Mrs Keeling! However, the fact remained that we were fellow East Enders who had moved a long way from home. It created a bond of sorts. The seeds of trust had been planted, and we forged a relationship where we could both work for Frankie's benefit.

During our initial meeting, I had been firm and direct, feeling that I could not appear to endorse threats of violence, even just by listening to them. However, over time, she learned to respect and trust me.

After a few weeks, I had another meeting with Mrs Keeling, this time for entirely positive reasons. I was delighted with the

Lesson 5 - Trust - Don't Stop Believin'

progress Frankie had made. When I first met him, he found handwriting very difficult, and both his presentation and the content of what he wrote were well below what is expected for a child of his age. The other TA in class, named Katy, and I, gave him the task of practising his handwriting for twenty minutes every morning shortly after arriving at school. If he did not match the level he had attained the previous day, or show slight improvement, he had to repeat the exercise. At first, he complained, but then accepted the challenge, and we praised every positive step he made.

Eventually, with a broad smile, he showed his writing to both the class and the deputy head. He was given a round of applause and a house point, and his mother was also very pleased when he proudly showed her his work after school.

The text in the left of the picture was the first piece of Frankie's writing I saw on the week I arrived at the school. The second piece was written just a few weeks later. The improvement is obvious. As well as being able to write neatly in cursive, he underlined the date and learning objective, and the content itself was full of excellent features. In just a few weeks, the TAs and I had made a difference! I strive to be proactive during each tenure and I am always eager to advance the children's learning in any way possible. This is further evidence that supply teachers can, and do, make a difference in a very short period of time.

Lesson 5 - Trust - Don't Stop Believin'

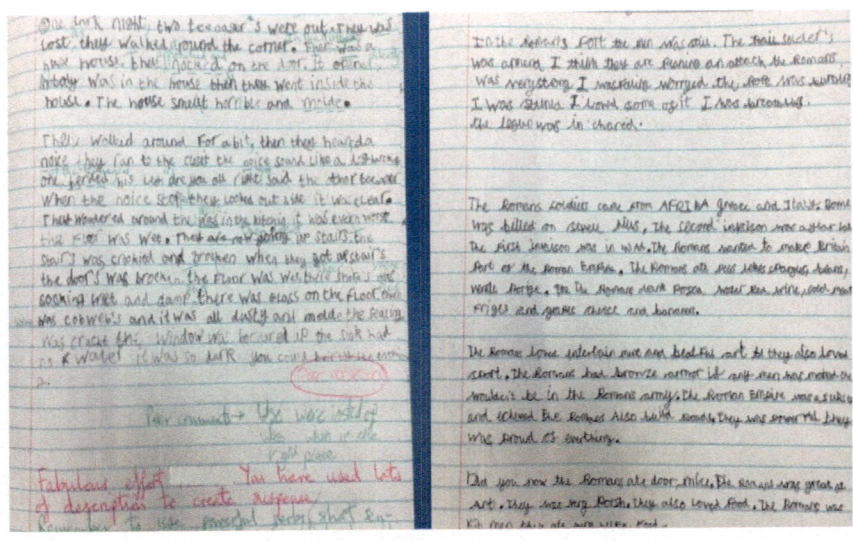

Other parents needed to address concerns with me too from time to time, and the headteacher at that same school referred to my ability to turn a situation around with a difficult parent as the, "Mr Kersey Magic." I recall him even asking me on one occasion to speak to the disgruntled parents of a child who was not even in my class or year group.

Every child needs to feel that any adult they confide in at school will take them seriously, and parents need to feel this too. It is important that they all know children's voices are heard at school. However, children are not always forthcoming with the whole truth in their reporting of incidents.

In early spring 2018, at the same school once again, I met with Mr and Mrs Regan, whose daughter, Melissa, was in my class.

They had unexpectedly arrived at the front office after school and wanted to see me right away. I knew that these parents had reduced another teacher to tears the previous year, after criticising her and shouting at her.

I quickly placed a few chairs out, and warmly greeted them as they entered the classroom. I invited them to sit down with me. Mr Regan looked very stern, but I listened to their concerns, and felt everything was fine as I answered their questions. Suddenly, Mr Regan blurted out, "And why did you keep Melissa inside at lunchtime today?" This took me completely by surprise. It seemed Melissa had misrepresented what had actually happened, so I gently called her over and asked her why she had spent some time in class during lunchtime. She looked a little embarrassed, and I explained to her parents what had happened. In a short period of time, it had become apparent to me that some children struggled to complete, or even start, their homework at home. This was sometimes because of a lack of parental support, and other times because they had not properly understood the assignment, which I would always explain in class – two or three times. In consultation with my TAs and the headteacher, I decided to offer help to any child who wanted it during my lunch break. It was not compulsory, but I wanted the children to feel free to approach me if they felt they needed extra help with their homework. They always had their meal first, of course, and since our time together was limited to ten or fifteen minutes, there was still plenty of time for them to play outside.

Lesson 5 - Trust - Don't Stop Believin'

As I explained this to Mr and Mrs Regan, and told them that I had to eat my large Cornish pasty as I helped Melissa that day, he laughed, amused perhaps at the image of her teacher scoffing a large pasty while teaching his daughter. I even pointed out the pastry flakes which were still scattered on the carpet by a child's table where I had eaten. Mr Regan again gave a little chuckle. I then turned to Melissa and said to her, "That's why you wanted to stay in, wasn't it, Melissa?" She nodded, and her dad smiled again. Like Mrs Keeling, Mr and Mrs Regan learned to trust me. This particular situation could easily have developed into a heated argument, but I always try to control my demeanour and what I say during misunderstandings or potential confrontations with parents. I control the situation, not them.

The importance of complete trustworthiness is ingrained in my thought processes. It is intrinsic with my position, and I am very conscious that the work will not come in if I cannot be trusted. However, careless talk can damage an honourable reputation. I learned this the hard way after making an innocent comment, which landed a colleague in a spot of bother.

This experience happened at another of my favourite schools, this time at a school in Bournemouth in 2019, where I had been working a few days each week, over a period of three to four months. The school had asked me to cover various age groups, but mostly Early Years and Key Stage One. One of the TAs in the Early Years group named Sandy, had needed some time off work with a virus, and after a brief return, suffered with some back trouble, and needed further time to rest. Unfortunately, shortly after returning to work, she then developed laryngitis, and was obliged to take more time off.

On a Friday evening, about a week before the Christmas holiday, I saw Sandy with her mother at the local shopping centre while I was out with my wife. We greeted them, and Sandy hoarsely whispered that she had laryngitis. We chatted briefly, I wished her a speedy recovery, and we went our separate ways.

The following Monday, during my lunch break in the staff room, I heard a colleague mention Sandy by name. I asked how she was, and unwittingly commented that she had been poorly with laryngitis when I saw her last Friday. I immediately knew I had made a mistake when the teacher she worked with, asked the first of several probing questions. It was an awkward situation, because I knew there had been some tension previously between Sandy and this teacher. Although I was honest, I also tried to defend Sandy, explaining that she did not sound well at all, and probably needed to just get outside for some fresh air. It was clear, however, that some of her workmates were very unhappy with Sandy.

As I was leaving school, the headteacher stopped me in the car park to confirm that I had seen Sandy at the shopping centre the previous Friday. I repeated what had happened and told him I felt awful if my innocent comment had caused trouble for her. He reassured me, told me not to worry, and thanked me for being honest.

Lesson 5 - Trust - Don't Stop Believin'

A few weeks later, my wife and I were enjoying picking up bargains in the January sales, and while I was waiting for her outside a shop, I saw Sandy and her mother again. I called her name and greeted her, but although both she and her mother smiled at me, they walked straight into the shop, and it was clear they did not want to speak to me. I assumed that she must have thought I had gone out of my way to get her into trouble, and although I wanted to sincerely apologise for my comment and clarify what had happened, I realised she would probably think I was just making excuses. I felt so guilt-ridden!

I hope if Sandy ever reads this, she will recognise this story and know that I am truly sorry that my innocent comment may have resulted in reproach or any discipline from the school. That was never my intention.

That experience was rare for me, as I generally try to be very careful while in conversation with colleagues and parents. Even so, I did wrong! I still regret that act of naivety to this day. Being aware and self-disciplined regarding what information I divulge to colleagues at school, and more importantly, to people outside of school, is crucial. It is so easy to get mixed up in loose talk at school, especially in the staff room because that is where I feel most relaxed, and therefore, it is easy to drop my guard and slip up.

In education, trust and reputation sets a positive precedence and foundation, and is absolutely paramount to safeguarding, fur-

Lesson 5 - Trust - Don't Stop Believin'

ther success for childrens' learning and all schools, and ultimately, more assignments for me.

Lesson 6

Positivity

Don't Worry, Be Happy

The most fruitful and optimum individuals are generally positive thinkers. They are dedicated and steadfast with reaching their goals, despite great opposition sometimes. I often share the following story to children in school, either in class or in an assembly, when the subject is about setting goals, determination and achieving success. It is a wonderful story.

I had the pleasure of meeting David Beckham's former PE teacher while working as a Schools' Liaison Officer (SLO) as a police constable, within the Youth and Community Section (YACS) of the Metropolitan Police Service between 1998 and 2000. I was allocated ten primary schools and three secondary schools in East London, and one of those high schools was where David Beckham attended.

David had left the school by the time I started teaching there, but interestingly, another future England football captain would also attend the same secondary school years later – Harry Kane. How remarkable for this school, that two England football captains attended their school.

While chatting with David's former PE teacher, whose name

Lesson 6 - Positivity - Don't Worry, Be Happy

I unfortunately cannot recall, so I will call him Mr Clark, I asked him to tell me something interesting about David. I wasn't looking for any kind of gossip, just curious to know what kind of pupil David was. Mr Clark shared the following.

He said that David was a very well-behaved student, who was an average pupil academically, but there was one particular subject in which he excelled at - PE. David enjoyed PE, and his specific passion was his determination to be a professional footballer. Whenever David was asked by educators what job he would like when he left school, he would always reply that he wanted to be a footballer.

Such was David's desire to succeed with his dream, that every day after school, either alone or with a friend or two, he would go to the school field, and practise set-pieces: bending free kicks, penalties, corners and crosses. In addition, Mr Clark said that David would practise in all weathers, and nothing deterred his quest. Consequently, with all the practising, he honed these skills to admirable applause. We are all familiar with the rest of David's extraordinary success story thereafter.

After sharing the above account at school, I then tell the children that we may not be a top mathematician, or a talented artist, or an astounding story writer, or a fantastic musician, but every one of us will be good at something. It could be a subject, a hobby, or even just a curious interest. Yet, if that is what we desire to do and become proficient at, then just like David Beckham, we should set goals, work hard and keep practising to achieve that success. I also remind the children, that with different talents and interests, it is another component which makes us all unique and diverse.

One of my responsibilities as a SLO was to prepare and teach lessons to these schools in East London. The lessons included subjects like the history of the police, stranger danger, drugs awareness, dangers of medicines, rights and responsibilities, and the consequences of crime.

I even performed several assemblies where I would dress up as a Victorian policeman, with a lantern, top hat, old tunic, fake sideburns, fake moustache, and a pillow stuffed up my shirt to make me look like a stereotypical, plump, old-fashioned bobby. Some of the artefacts were borrowed from the Metropolitan Police Museum, and I always ensured all borrowed items were looked after carefully and returned on time.

The lessons and assemblies were so much fun! It was during this time that I received many compliments about my teaching style from teachers and headteachers. I was often asked if I had taught before and whether I was interested in becoming a teacher. I wasn't to know then that my journey would wind its way to me eventually qualifying as a schoolteacher over ten years later.

Lesson 6 - Positivity - Don't Worry, Be Happy

Me as a Victorian Policeman - circa 1899. Oops! I mean 1999.

Upon leaving the police service, I was a house husband for our two little girls, until we emigrated to Australia. Once we arrived in Australia, I proactively considered a new career, and decided to train to be a schoolteacher. However, I did not have the qualifications to enter university, so I embarked on a year's study at a local TAFE (Technical and Further Education) in Australia to gain the necessary qualifications (the equivalent of UK 'A' Levels) for university. That was an interesting experience to say the least.

Every Thursday, I would attend a four-hour English lesson, then nip across the road to a snug shopping mall for a bite to eat, before a four-hour maths lesson in the evening. The English lessons were very enjoyable, though I did have to study intensely. Having a gifted teacher was a huge bonus for me because she pushed me and pushed me onto success. I was subsequently rewarded with an 'A+' in my final exam. My English teacher emailed me to congratulate me on my results and called me the 'Dux of the Class.'

On the other hand, maths was a 'different kettle of fish.' This was higher level maths which I was studying, and the lessons would give me headaches – something I rarely suffer with.

The learning, to begin with, was way above my head. It didn't help the situation when I turned up for the first lesson and pulled out a $5 calculator that I had purchased from one of the stalls at the local market. I soon discovered that everyone in class had these large 'scientific' calculators, which came with an equally cumbersome instruction manual. I had never heard of a scientific calculator up to that point. I had read in the welcome pack that I needed to purchase a scientific calculator. But aren't all calculators scientific? I thought at the time – so I went to the market to buy a cheap calculator! I felt a right nitwit!

I soon befriended two young Greek students who were also on the same course. They were extremely encouraging and friendly towards me and helped me with any questions. One was named Arthur (not the most common Greek name I know) and an amateur boxer. I wished I had kept in touch with both of them when I completed the course a year later. They were a great support to me!

Such was the initial struggle with the maths learning, that my wife suggested I hire a tutor. We soon found a middle-aged maths tutor named Willy, who was good at his job but swore like a

Lesson 6 - Positivity - Don't Worry, Be Happy

trooper. I persevered with the course and subsequently earned a 'C' grade. I now had the qualifications, which would eventually allow me to enter university.

Once I had successfully gained these qualifications, I was unfortunately not in a position to enter University in Australia, due to financial reasons, with my wife expecting our third child. So, I became an estate agent in Australia. My accent seemed to open a lot of doors and opportunities for listing and selling property.

After five years in Australia, we arrived back in the UK. Seventeen months later, and after our youngest child had started formal schooling, I was finally able to study for a degree in Primary education and commence my teacher training at university.

Those three years, while studying to qualify as a teacher, were extremely challenging, and we were beset with all kinds of hurdles to overcome. My wife worked full-time as a teacher, our eldest child had seven operations for cancer treatment, and we were harassed by local yobs for about sixteen months. These perpetrators, wearing balaclavas and hoodies, created wanton acts of anti-social behaviour, including kicking and banging on our front door late at night, and hurling stones, rocks and dog poo at our front door and windows. On top of all that, we lived in three different properties: two in Essex and one in Dorset - an approximate three-hour car drive from Essex. The original plan had been to relocate to Dorset from Essex after I had qualified as a teacher. However, the constant harassment from the local youths in Essex forced our hand, and we had to quickly move one year earlier from our own home and into rented accommodation.

Consequently, and during my final year at university, I would drive to Essex on a Sunday evening to stay with friends for a few days, in order to attend my lectures, before returning home on Wednesday evening. Two days later, I would arise at 4am, and drive to Essex once again, in order to attend a one-hour lecture. Remote learning was unavailable at the time, and I had promised my university lecturers that I wouldn't miss any lectures if we moved to Dorset. In that final year, I only missed one lecture due to illness. It was a very financially expensive (house moving and fuel costs especially) and torrid time for us all as a young family, and I could so easily have walked away from the studying and teacher training.

In 2011, despite extremities mostly beyond our control, over the previous few years, I qualified as a teacher. If you want dreams to come true, then be undaunted in your pursuit -despite the sacrifices and hardships. Rarely does anything of great worth just present itself on a plate – unless you are very fortunate. You must dream then do!

Creating a positive atmosphere in class is vital, and there are a number of things that I can prepare for and introduce in class, which all supports this positive environment. Occasionally, I have to think 'outside the box' when no plans or resources have been left, or I have entered an unfamiliar setting. Good supply teachers can cope with 'hitting the ground running' whatever the age group they have been requested to teach. Whether arriving early, or perhaps delayed due to that late call from the agency, they can 'pick up the threads' of the learning that is going on in class. They are able to evaluate the children and their learning very quickly, effecting a smooth transition in spite of any adverse circumstances. I always aspire to be that kind of supply teacher whenever I visit a school, and I know that I must be mentally prepared and organised for the cover role, whether I will be there for just a day or for several weeks or months.

Firstly, experience has taught me several key factors when faced with the scenario of having no plans or resources at hand, when the teacher is absent. I check to see if there is a TA assigned to that class, and if not, then perhaps another member of staff within the same year group. If no TA or teacher is available to chat with, then perhaps the deputy head or a member of the senior leadership team can advise me. It is imperative to build a healthy working relationship with these adults as quickly as possible. I ask them about seating arrangements, especially for children with specific needs, and make a note of prior learning as well as daily routines and child monitors. I find out which children can be trusted to take messages, and what behaviour management techniques the school favours and also what reward system is used in the class. Keeping to established routines as far as possible is desirable, as making changes can affect children's confidence and focus. It is important to keep disruption to a minimum.

Secondly, a brief perusal of the children's maths, English and topic books, if time is permitted, will inform me regarding the subjects the children have been studying. Additionally, I check if there was cover for the previous day or week. If so, I look for a feedback sheet from that cover teacher, as the information there can be helpful to me as well as to the class teacher.

Furthermore, I don't like to be bereft of resources, so I take a selection of maths and English worksheets for various age groups in case I find myself in a situation where no plans or material have been left for me. I also keep a memory stick with me, so that I have a variety of maths, English, science and topic PowerPoints, and other resources to draw on if the need arises.

Also, the transition from break or lunchtime to and from the classroom can be chaotic. If the school or class routine allows, I like to line the children up and remind them to leave and enter the classroom quietly. I inform them what the learning will be, prior to re-entering the classroom, and where I want them to sit, such as their carpet spot if they are younger children. This short period of adjustment works wonders in creating a controlled environment after all the running around in the playground, and perhaps the screaming and squabbles too. A calm and happy atmosphere is a positive atmosphere!

Finally, if I have a spare moment at the end of the day, reading to the class is another productive way of settling the children down. Occasionally, I like to invite the younger children to lie down on the carpet after they have collected their home time items, so they can chill as I read to them. This also creates a settled and positive envi-

Lesson 6 - Positivity - Don't Worry, Be Happy

ronment, and an ideal way to quieten the children after the hustle and bustle of any pushing and shoving when gathering home time things in the corridor. It is reassuring to parents and carers to find their children composed and happy when they collect them, rather than hyperactive, tearful or sometimes, in complete madness!

For any educator visiting a school for the very first time, it can be a challenge to develop positive relationships with the children in class straight away – but it is possible! With the right techniques, body language, facial expressions, tone of voice, empathy, praise and appropriate humour, it can be done almost immediately. From my experience, children will respond better to me if they like me and trust me. I try to build positive relationships while implementing the classroom rules!

I fondly recall one lunch time, while teaching at a school in Boscombe, when a Year Six boy named Ben, who had behavioural challenges, approached me in the playground and asked if I would be teaching his class that afternoon. "No, I'm sorry, Ben," I said, "I'm in Year Five all day today." Looking forlorn, he bounced a ball in front of me. I then asked him if he would like me to teach him that day, to which he smiled, and quietly muttered, "Yes."

I had first taught Ben a few weeks previously for just one day, and I had been warned not to confront him if he kicked off, but to allow the TA to deal with him. She would then remove him from the class if necessary. However, the TA had to go home sick in the morning, so I was on my own.

Lesson 6 - Positivity - Don't Worry, Be Happy

Ben was aloof and arrogant, so I used positivity and praise, and gently reminded him of boundaries. At lunchtime, the children ate in the classroom, and I chose to sit next to Ben to mark the books, while he tucked into his lunch. I asked him about his interests outside school, and he told me that he had a pet African pygmy hedgehog at home. I explored this interest with him, and he showed me an image of one on the Internet. He seemed comfortable with me as I showed regard for him. Now, three weeks later, he wanted me back in his class to teach him for the day. It was very pleasing to know. I shared this with one of the Year Five teachers, who said that for Ben to want a certain supply teacher to return, was very impressive.

As I left school, I told the business manager about my moment with Ben. She responded, "When we need a supply teacher, we always ask for you now." I truly believe in the power of nurturing self-esteem, confidence, independence and creativity in children. Engaging with their interests is one way of showing a child that you genuinely care. That genuine care is also what I have seen displayed by numerous educators over the years too.

The learning environment I try to create in class, is also an engaging environment, where children thrive in their learning. More importantly, it is an environment where children can feel happy and safe.

I recall with fondness, a day spent with a Year One class at a school in Poole in 2015. It was Pirate Day for all the Year One children, and I had received a late call from the agency, and therefore had to tackle the heavy traffic. Within minutes of walking into class, and having just a few minutes to familiarise myself with the planning and activities for the day ahead, the children, all excited and wearing colourful and extravagant pirate costumes, were arriving. As I sat the children down on the carpet and read out the register in my best pirate accent, which resembled more of a West Country brogue, the TA was literally dressing me in pirate attire, which they had managed to find in the school. I was 'hitting the peddle to the metal.' Shiver me timbers indeed! Nevertheless, I remained cheerful and happy. I was in the moment and enjoyed the occasion immensely, even though my journey and arrival had been very hectic to begin with.

I wrote a poem about that fun day, a few years later. The TA took a photo of me in costume, which I have included after the poem.

"Up at the crack of dawn
Showered, dressed, no time to yawn
Keen and raring to go
No call! What a blow.

What's this? A call at eight
That traffic will surely make me late
Arrive at the office with a smile
Ready to go the extra mile.

Walk into the classroom setting
Totally calm with no fretting
Despite only six minutes to scan
The teacher notes and daily learning plan.

Pirates' Day I'm told
Just as the children come in from the cold
TA dressing me in pirate attire
As I read the register, right on the wire.

Practise our pirate voice
Shiver me timbers, what a noise
An intro of our pirate gear
Providing such a fun atmosphere.

Now, all hands on deck
Let's get this pirate maths in check
Superb pirate story writing
No! Let's not have any pirate biting.

Pirate art is a must
My wonky pirate braids need to adjust
Sing-a-long to some pirate tunes
Laughter while watching pirate cartoons.

Lesson 6 - Positivity - Don't Worry, Be Happy

Aarrgghh, lunchtime arrives
Well deserved high fives
Batten down the hatches
I'm a pirate joining in some football matches.

Afternoon learning, Ahoy, me hearties
Let's have a fabulous pirate party
Pirate games excite and abound
The child in me has today been found."

- By Grant J. Kersey
  4th October 2020

As a pirate for Year One Pirate Day in 2016.

Lesson 6 - Positivity - Don't Worry, Be Happy

Educators are often pleasantly surprised that I have remembered their name when I haven't seen them for an extended period. That is because I implemented a habit, in my first year of supplying, by recording staff names on my smartphone. As I park my car upon arrival at a school, I get my smartphone out and check details of staff names I had previously recorded. I remind myself of the names of the office staff, the headteacher and deputy head, as well as the teachers and TAs in the year group I will be working in that day. Where possible, I will even record the names of the cleaners and lunchtime supervisors. Everyone you encounter at school deserves to be recognised and respected. A great quote I came across during my research for this book is from the British actor, Tom Hardy, who said, "I was raised to treat the janitor with the same respect as the CEO."[11] That's the attitude to have at work and in life! Everyone matters!

While the cleaner is wiping down the tables or vacuuming the classroom, I am mindful of their duties. There may not be sufficient room at the teacher's desk to mark that high pile of books, so perhaps I am sitting at one of the children's tables. If the cleaner does walk in, I ask them politely whether I need to move for them. Most often, they will be courteous and tell me that where I am sitting is fine, but I still ask. I'm sure they appreciate that thoughtful gesture. When I then greet colleagues by name, whom I haven't seen for a while, they are often pleasantly surprised and impressed that I have remembered their name. Of course, changes of staff are inevitable, so I record such changes for next time.

Lesson 6 - Positivity - Don't Worry, Be Happy

Schools know that I am confident teaching any age group, and as a result, I am prepared for any assignment that comes my way. The greater variation of work I confidently accept, the more popular and useful I am with each school and my agency.

Although I am ready to accept any assignment, now and then I am stretched a bit too far – or so it may seem initially. This happened when I was at a school in Bournemouth in January 2019. It is a good school with both primary and secondary children on one site. While I was waiting to be met by Mr Day, the deputy head, I overheard him speaking to the receptionist over the radio. He told her I would be teaching music to secondary students all day. Panic set in! Music? All day? To secondary students? The only thing I can play is the radio!

When I eventually met Mr Day, neither he nor the teacher he sent me to speak with knew what material I was supposed to be teaching. I had twenty minutes to organise something, so headed to the music room in the hope that I would find a lesson plan. But no! There was nothing! Moreover, there were no musical instruments either. Would I have to hunt for them too? Panic set in further. This was crazy! I thought.

Finally, with about ten minutes remaining before the children arrived, I discovered, much to my relief, that I would only be teaching two written music lessons in the geography room, and would be finished teaching music by lunchtime. Luckily for me, the subject was the history of modern music since the 1950s. I love eclectic music genres, especially from the 1950s, 60s and 70s so everything had panned out perfectly for me. Despite the initial confusion and delay, I had kept smiling and had remained outwardly calm and confident, even if I had felt like a 'flapping fish out of water' to begin with.

Children can change the way we look at life so that we are inspired to care better for our world, each other, and importantly, ourselves. If we allow such changes to take place, we can become more teachable, more thoughtful, more gentle and more compassionate. Children can help us to reach our potential to be better adults.

In May 2019, I was working in a Year Two class at a school in Bournemouth. I met twin brothers, Jack and Toby, both of whom had the most beautiful natures. They were severely visually impaired, and wore thick rimmed glasses, and although the school had made extra provisions and adjustments in the classroom to accommodate their particular needs, such as computer monitors at the front of the classroom for them to look at during 'carpet time,' they continued to have difficulty reading texts. They would put books and worksheets within inches of their eyes so that they could see the words. However, they went about their tasks almost silently and never complained.

Both boys were highly intelligent, and their writing and understanding of mathematics were outstanding. I felt they had promising futures, despite their obvious challenges. Nevertheless, I couldn't help wondering about the trials of life that faced them as they made their way in an uncompromising and sometimes harsh world. I wondered to what extent their condition might deteriorate, whether treatment might be available to stop the degenerative condition, and how relationships, friendships or career prospects might be affected. I noticed that when they played outside, although they would initially join in with the other children, they soon found themselves on the periphery, with just each other for company. Although they each had one-on-one support, I found myself periodically checking on their progress, and felt overwhelming compassion for them. Whenever I asked if they were okay, they would look at me, squinting their eyes and just smile. Their polite, yet shy demeanour was endearing and enigmatic. I was very touched by their positive outlook on life, as well as by how they treated others, and positively coped with their own disabilities.

Teaching Jack and Toby caused me to reflect on my own eyesight. I was fifty three years old, and had been complaining to my wife that I now needed reading glasses, an expense that consistently had low priority in our budgeting. Knowing Jack and Toby humbled me, and put my own situation into perspective. After all, most of us can expect some degree of failing eyesight as we age. In comparison with the challenges these boys faced for the rest of their lives, my little problem faded into insignificance.

Sometimes in class, the teacher becomes the student. Jack and Toby made a strong, positive and indelible impression on me during my time at that school.

Lesson 6 - Positivity - Don't Worry, Be Happy

Two months later, I returned to that school to teach another class. While taking a few children to the office at the end of the school day, I saw these twins with their mother. I approached the mum and said, "Excuse me, my name is Mr Kersey. I taught your two boys a couple of months ago, and they are two of the most delightful children I have ever taught." I then put my arm around one of them and crouching down, I said, "They probably don't remember me, but I remember them. They are so sweet and polite." Their mum thanked me and said, "I bet they do remember you. Boys do you remember Mr Kersey?" With warm smiles, they both looked up at me and nodded. Again, my heart was touched by these two beautiful souls with such a positive outlook to life and their personal challenges.

Radiating a happy and positive energy makes a real difference in all schools. I was thrilled to hear that the half term topic in the spring of 2018, at a fabulous school in mid-Dorset, was the Romans. What a great subject to teach the children! I knew the learning would be both informative and enjoyable.

In the final week of our topic learning, the class put on an assembly for their parents and the entire school. I was eager for this to be a superb assembly and following weeks of detailed planning and rehearsals, I was keen for the children to give a polished performance. It would be a show of shows!

The assembly included a face off battle scene between Ancient Britons and Roman centurions to the music of Fat Boy Slim's

Lesson 6 - Positivity - Don't Worry, Be Happy

hit, Right Here, Right Now, which I had choreographed. Several children proudly presented their own astounding written work, and a PowerPoint presentation, which I had created and based on Queen's iconic image, was also shared. I changed the word 'Rock' to 'Rome' and replaced the image of the legendary Freddie Mercury with that of a Roman emperor. I had added corny jokes and plenty of interesting and unusual facts in the script I had also written.

The first slide from my PowerPoint Presentation

Finally, we ended with a fun song I had personally written. I wanted a tune the audience would know very well, so I chose YMCA. The words were added to a PowerPoint slide in order to spur the audience into joining in with the sing along. Here are the words I wrote:

Lesson 6 - Positivity - Don't Worry, Be Happy

Verse 1:
"Claudius, there's no need to feel down
We said, Claudius, you must be so proud
We said, Claudius, 'cos you found a country
There's no need to be so grumpy.

Verse 2:
Claudius, you built lots of roads
We said, Claudius, we saw a new mode
We said, Claudius, those baths made us clean
Thanks for showing us some hygiene.

Chorus:
You conquered Britain in 43 A.D.
You conquered Britain in 43 A.D.
We have tin and iron and lots of gold to try
Though the weather will make you cry.
You conquered Britain in 43 A.D.
You conquered Britain in 43 A.D."
(Fade music out)

- By Grant J. Kersey

April 2018

Lesson 6 - Positivity - Don't Worry, Be Happy

After the show, I had a deep feeling of euphoria. We had created a production that had been enchanting, popular and successful. The children had excelled themselves and I was immensely proud of each and every one of them. One of my TAs, Sharna, said to me afterwards, that in the five years she had worked at the school, this class assembly was the best she had ever seen. The head-teacher, Mr Carson, would later describe it as, "…something out of Hollywood!" in a reference for me. I still wax lyrical about that assembly. It was a marvellous and positive experience for everyone.

About two months later, and still at the same school, I was the designated adult in charge of a brilliant trip to Weymouth Sailing Club. This was the same sailing centre where the sailing events during the London 2012 Olympics took place. The activity for the children that day was paddleboarding. This school really knew how to put on exciting activities and day trips for its children, and this was one of the most fantastic I have ever been involved with.

However, this particular day could so easily have ended as a catastrophe, with a terrible injury to someone. Prior to the children attempting paddleboarding, the instructors had gathered all the children in a shallow area of water (about waist deep for the adults) and engaged the children in various running and clambering activities in the water. A few educators were in the water too, including me. As we joined in the fun, I suddenly trod on an object that was so sharp that it pierced the hard sole of one of my aqua shoes, and I felt a sharpened twinge touch the sole of my foot. I put

Lesson 6 - Positivity - Don't Worry, Be Happy

my hand in the water and pulled out a piece of pointed driftwood, which had been vertically sticking out of the seabed, like a weever fish's venomous spine waiting for an unsuspecting victim to tread on it. I was grateful that miraculously, it was I who had trodden on the piece of sharp wood, and not one of the children or colleagues in bare feet. I don't believe that it was just sheer coincidence, that it was me, wearing strong aqua shoes, who just happened to tread on that sharp piece of driftwood that day. It was so sharp that it would have pierced through any bare foot with ease. I was very grateful that there were no accidents and injuries, and we all had such a memorable and positive experience on that warm and sunny day.

Paddleboarding school trip to Weymouth Sailing Club in June 2018.

On the return journey, I sat at the front of the hired coach opposite the driver. We decided a sing-a-long would help entertain everyone, so I took the microphone and asked for requests. One of the children immediately asked for YMCA and they all spontaneously sang my lyrics rather than the original version. I didn't even have to ask them to sing my lyrics. It was very satisfying!

That entire seven-month placement, despite a two-and-a-half hour round trip every day, became one of my most pleasurable tenures. There is no better feeling in teaching than when you are loving and enjoying your job. It makes all the demands and effort worth it. The experiences at that mid-Dorset school were indeed a truly positive and thoroughly delightful one for me.

I am continually impressed, that despite underfunding and financial constraints for many schools, educators, together with school governors, parent support groups and even the local community, seek opportunities to provide an assortment of extra-curricular activities for children. This may be in the form of lunchtime and after school clubs, school trips, or guest visitors to the school. These initiatives are primarily designed to allow children to experience a variety of learning, including the arts, hobbies, crafts and sports, while simultaneously enhancing either existing skills, or awakening new skills in the child. It is often the school that bears the brunt of most of the expenses incurred. Government could do well to listen to the voices being echoed by schools around the country: give schools a greater budget to cope with the ever-in-

Lesson 6 - Positivity - Don't Worry, Be Happy

creasing burdens and high expectations.

While in my last year at university, I completed a series of paintings as part of the course. My final piece was very symbolic and had deep meaning.

I had visited London sometime in 2010, with the intention of taking photographs of a rally by educators and their supporters. They were demonstrating against cuts in education funding, proposals for significant increases in tuition fees and other related matters. While there, I also took photos of the police officers who were monitoring and policing the event. Soon afterwards, I felt inspired to create a work of art, which depicted myself, as such, protesting against continual government cutbacks in education. I became the police officers protesting in the painting.

Police Protesting Against Educational Cuts by Grant J. Kersey

Symbolic references within the painting are dark clouds of trouble heading our way; Big Ben as the big brother peering over our shoulder; the public talking to a brick wall; and people's hopes fading away with the insubstantial fire gradually burning out.

I still own this large canvas, though it is a little mouldy now, having lived its life in our loft, garage, under the bed, and now currently hidden under the stairs! Finding a 'home' within our home for such a large painting has been a challenge to say the least – but I refuse to dispose of it!

Government needs to listen more genuinely and intently, and act positively to help educators and schools meet the ever-increasing demands placed upon them, through satisfactory school budgets and better pay conditions. As they do so, schools will be even more productive in providing the staff and resources to provide an even higher quality of education and support to all children, especially those with special needs. I'm sure that the mental health of educators would benefit too.

Now, wouldn't that just be the ultimate teamwork scenario with government ministers being in the 'same league' as educators?

Lesson 7

Teamwork

We Are The Champions

I love to embrace individualism. When I am tasked with completing a task independently, I am generally optimistic about it. However, there is only so much I can achieve on my own and a framework for success at school is built upon several elements, including teamwork. Supply teachers are just as important to the day-to-day operations of a school as any other member of staff, and every person plays a key role in the school's success: each a vital 'cog in the wheel' so to speak.

Schools build their success on the team of educators all pulling together, and I always look for opportunities to support colleagues, stepping in immediately if the situation demands. Teachers are inundated with a never-ending workload, and there are always boxes to tick, people to see, forms to fill, reports to complete, work to be checked, lessons resources to prepare and set up and innumerable other jobs to be completed.

If I know that my lesson resources are all set up and ready for the entire morning, and I have familiarised myself with the planning, and I haven't been asked to be on duty at breaktime, I make a habit of offering to do someone else's break duty; a gesture my colleagues always appreciate. It is further evidence of getting involved and being a team player.

While working at a school in Bournemouth, I was fulfilling a lunchtime duty in the dining room, when I saw a Year Two boy barging past the other children. He raced to the front of the queue as all the children entered from the playground. One of the lunchtime supervisors saw his appalling behaviour and asked him to go back to the entrance and to walk into the hall sensibly and quietly. He smirked at her, ignored her instruction and stayed where he was at the front of the queue.

Seeing the potential for a teaching moment, and also to support a colleague, I approached the miscreant and calmly said, "Excuse me, young man. You have been asked by one of the lunchtime supervisors to go back to the door and walk in sensibly. You have deliberately ignored her. Now, please go and show her, and me, that you can walk in quietly."

Without making a fuss, he did just that. I praised and thanked him for following my instruction. I reminded him also, that he needed to follow instructions from all adults within the school. The dinner ladies thanked me for intervening and that was the end of the matter. In this case, my intervention was successful. However, I was not aware of the child's background or any established steps for his behaviour. Hence, the need to be tactful and careful when dealing with disruptive children whom I am not familiar with.

Lesson 7 - Teamwork - We Are The Champions

In September 2019, I was teaching a pleasant Year Two class for the day at another school in Bournemouth. I noticed that the half-term topic for that year was Roald Dahl's, Fantastic Mr Fox. The teacher had created the beginnings of a large topic display and had already began exhibiting the children's work. I noticed that there was a large gap in the centre of the display. I enquired about the reason for the gap and the teacher explained that she had not been able to find a suitably large image of Fantastic Mr Fox as the centre piece of the display. The images were always far too small. I offered to sketch an image on an A2 flipchart sheet during my lunchbreak. She was initially hesitant and felt that this would be too much to expect from a supply teacher, but I insisted that I was happy to help. The sketch was finished by the end of my lunch break. The teacher was thrilled and grateful for my input, and fortunately felt my sketch was good enough to add to the display. I was delighted that I had been able to use my artistic talents to benefit her, the children, and the classroom.

My quick sketch of Fantastic Mr Fox

Lesson 7 - Teamwork - We Are The Champions

Another fond memory I hold dear to my heart, occurred at a school in Hampshire. A few weeks before the Easter break, I was asked if I would be interested in setting up an extra-curricular lunchtime or after-school club. I declined the offer because to me that just meant extra work, on top of an already busy agenda. Nonetheless, it became apparent to me that there was an after-school football club for the Year Five and Six boys, but there was nothing for the Year Three and Four boys. The younger boys were missing out!

After the Easter break, I spoke to the headteacher, and made her aware that I had decided to set up an after-school football club for these Year Three and Year Four boys. She was thrilled with my decision. I asked a colleague, Tom, who worked in the resource provision of the school, to help me. He was hugely popular with the children and a great asset to the school. I was pleased that he was keen to join me. We advertised the club and sent out letters to parents, and soon had twenty boys enrolled in our club.

We trained every Thursday, and after we had warmed up and practised a variety of skills, there was always time for a match. The boys had a great time, as did Tom and I.

I found the response to the club, from some of the boys having very challenging behavioural problems, particularly remarkable. One of those boys was a lad named Jason, who had only been in the UK a short time. His family were from South Africa, and Jason was a strong kid who had displayed significant anger issues at school. Contrarily, during our practises and matches, he was a different child: composed and considerate. I never once witnessed him losing his temper. Even when he was tackled awkwardly or his team was losing, Jason maintained control of his temperament. Furthermore, when another player was injured, he would show concern and compassion for them. Tom and I were quick to praise him, and all his teammates, for their exemplary behaviour. We were proud of them all.

During one game, Jason's team was losing 4-0. His teammates had dropped their heads and were frustrated. They bickered and complained amongst themselves. Jason, however, without any prompting, motivated them to keep going. The team went on to score six goals, and although the final score was 7-6 to the other side, Tom and I recognised the team's huge achievement, as well as the leadership potential Jason had shown. It is inspiring to see that kind of positive mentality, especially in a child. Even when the odds are stacked against them, such individuals, including adults, rise above it all. They don't whinge or gossip! They are hopeful, helpful and co-operative.

The boys expressed a desire to play against another school, so Tom and I set up a match. We needed a captain for our team, and during one of our briefings, I asked Tom who he felt should be the team captain. He put forward the name of Jason, and I agreed wholeheartedly. Jason had consistently showed great leadership qualities every week. Jason was very happy with his new assignment.

Lesson 7 - Teamwork - We Are The Champions

The boys won their first game 12-0. We had instructed the boys to shake hands with their opponents at the end of the match, whatever the score. Jason ensured that his team did just that. Such acts of kindness from our boys showed great respect and maturity. I even saw a few of our boys hugging the other team, and I found it all so heart-warming.

The team went on to win their two other games too. Near the end of the summer term, the team all stood in assembly. Jason, as the captain, proudly introduced his team, and each boy reported one of the exciting moments of their final game to the whole school. I listened to their individual reports, feeling immensely honoured to have been part of their achievement, and especially proud of Jason. He had stood out, accepting the role of leading and motivating his team during football practises and matches against other schools. I made sure that he knew I was proud of him. Interestingly, while he was the team captain, I don't recall hearing of any behaviour problems reported by any of the staff. To raise someone up is to tell him you believe in them. Perhaps Jason craved recognition and care, and Tom and I gave that to him. We believed in Jason, and we trusted him, and he didn't once let us down.

Most schools always need to raise funds, and sponsored events, fairs and fetes are fun ways to achieve this, as well as bringing the school and local community together. Once again, if the circumstances permit, I like to get involved whenever possible.

While I was still at the same school, the staff were given a list of events for the forthcoming summer school fair. We were invited to choose which activity we would be responsible for. All the boxes were quickly filled, with the exception of one - the dreaded stocks. With no warning, an email was sent to all the staff from a teacher, who incidentally became the best teacher I have ever worked with. His name was Mark Rossow, and he was an all-round nice bloke. In the email, Mark said, "Grant has volunteered to go in the stocks!" I hadn't volunteered at all, but saw the funny side to the message, and wasn't about to shy away from the challenge. Mark had himself volunteered the previous year so now it was my turn. I began to anticipate experiencing what Medieval folk would have been subjected to for minor infringements of the law. I would be 'punished' in the stocks at the forthcoming school fair!

    I chose to wear my smart school clothes, rather than shorts and a t-shirt, so that children wanting to take their revenge, could do so on someone who dressed like a teacher! Strangely, my stall attracted the most people. I wonder why? Children, and parents alike, were keen to throw large, soggy, wet sponges at me. I egged them on with taunts of, "Losers!" and, "You'll miss me, even from there!" If they did miss, I blew a raspberry and shouted, "What a load of rubbish!" That just spurred them on, and many returned for a second or third attempt. Teasing others attracted a crowd, and crowds meant more participants, which ultimately meant more funds for the school coffers. This was my intention of course. It was a fund-raiser after all!

    Having had enough of my teasing and taunting, several children and mums, decided to walk right up to me and squeeze water over my head, allowing the water to trickle slowly down my neck and back. One mum so thoughtfully whispered to me, "This is what you get for giving my son a good report!" My goodness! I'd hate to think what my punishment would have been had I given her son a bad report. I was secretly loving the occasion.

An hour or two later, with a very sore neck, an aching lower back and sodden head to foot, I was thankfully released from my enclosure. Apparently, other than the popular BBQ, my event raised the most funds for the school that day. Job done!

In the stocks!

Depending upon the circumstances and my length of time at a school, I may be expected to take on other responsibilities too, such as report writing, end of term assessments, data input,

Lesson 7 - Teamwork - We Are The Champions

organising and marking test papers and parents' evenings. I have been involved in all these tasks, including a few parents' evenings, as a supply teacher.

One evening, at a school in mid-Dorset, the headteacher, Mr Carson, and a Year Six teacher, decided to sit in on one parents' evening, as a show of support for me, having only been at the school a few weeks. After the fourth set of parents, the headteacher quietly suggested to the Year Six teacher, that she was not needed because, "...Grant has this under control." I was not aware of this comment at the time, as it was made while I was greeting the next set of parents at the classroom door.

The following day, the Year Six teacher came up to me and shared her impressions from the evening before. She told me that I had a lovely way with the parents. I knew Mr Carson had better things to do with his time and reassured him that he needn't be at the second parents' evening, unless he wanted to. That evening, Mr Carson knew he wasn't needed and felt confident leaving that session solely to me.

There are other situations that allow further scope to get involved and be a team player at school. In November 2017, I arrived early in the morning at a school in Poole. The teacher, who was heading off for a course, briefly went through the timetable for the day. This included a 'mile a day' challenge, which she had recently introduced to her class. Great idea! I thought. Get those kids running outside, even if it is a bit chilly. After lunch, and to my surprise, the children informed me that the teacher always joined in with the run too. So, When in Rome, do as the Romans do! Unfortunately, I had no trainers, but without hesitation, I removed my tie, and explained to the children that I didn't want to show off by running ahead of them, as they'd be 'eating my dust.' I offered to run at the back so that I could observe them. I assured them I was nothing if not considerate!

After just four laps around the field and playground, with several children passing me, I felt I had put on a good show. It was all worth it when one young man said, "I love your amazing humour Mr Kersey. Are you coming back tomorrow?" "Sadly not," I replied. "I'm teaching my wife's Year One class!"

I don't want you to think that I shy away from physical fitness. It's just harder to keep up with those energetic and enthusiastic children when running those laps with them as I get older.

I have a passion for teaching PE in schools because I am aware of some of the health benefits for children. Young people who exercise regularly, can enjoy extensive health benefits, including vitality, better concentration, improved posture, balance and coordination, maintaining a healthy weight and building strong bones and muscles.

Physical fitness and eating healthily was important to me in my youth, although it may not be so obvious now with the 'insulation' keeping my six-pack warm! PE was one of my favourite subjects at school. I regularly ran long distances and when I was 14, together with a friend named Nick Chapman, I joined a gym.

Lesson 7 - Teamwork - We Are The Champions

A couple of evenings a week we would board either the 25 or 86 bus from Ilford, and travel to a gym in Stratford, East London. In those days, we had no fancy smoothies and there were very few choices of protein drinks available. Tap water in glass milk bottles was the only drink available at the gym, and I recall the gym equipment being mostly free-weights. The floor was just concrete with no cushioning, and I don't remember there being showers either. It was definitely a hard-core environment, yet I was surrounded by rugged cockneys, who appeared cultivated in the way they conversed and treated each other. I felt a sense of toughness just being in the company of these physically strong men - albeit a skinny version of them!

The proprietor of that gym, Bill Stevens, was a bodybuilder himself, and knew my maternal grandfather, Bill Oakes. Bill's parents were good friends with my granddad from their East End days. Years later, Bill Stevens, the gym proprietor, naturally treated me like royalty once he discovered who my maternal grandfather was.

With my interests in bodybuilding and art in my mid-teens, I drew (not traced) two images of famous bodybuilders at the time (Arnold Schwarzenegger and Franco Columbu) from a monthly bodybuilding magazine I used to buy. The date of each drawing is shown in the top left corner of each image. Decades later, I laminated and framed these drawings, so as to preserve them longer, and placed them on the wall of my home gym in the garage, which I had at the time.

Lesson 7 - Teamwork - We Are The Champions

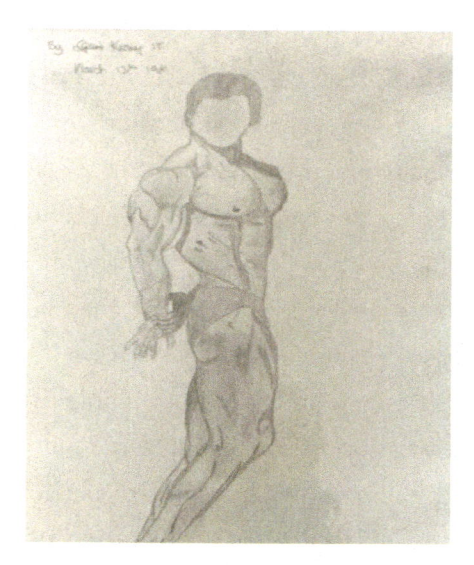

My sketch of Franco Columbu

My sketch of Arnold Schwarzenegger

Surprisingly, I have noticed that too many children complain when they have a pin prick cut or the slightest of abrasions. Many try and find any excuse to get out of participating in PE, or indeed breaktimes, especially when the temperature outside has dropped. A little pain for kids can be good for them! Having said that, I always establish whether any of the children have pre-existing conditions or injuries before a PE lesson and ask for advice from another adult in dealing with them if that is the case. Such children are reminded to make me aware if they are unable to participate with the activity, and where possible, I like to see a note from parents. If they do have a slight injury but wish to participate, then I am mindful of that too, and will go easy on them during the lesson. In spite of my persuasive encouragement and obvious desire for every child to have a go, I am not some uncompromising 'Miss Trunchbull' type! I care about each child's individual needs and endeavour to differentiate my PE expectations according to their abilities. If I know a child can run very fast, then I expect to see that. I want every child to just do their best.

As a consequence, I take my PE lessons very seriously and encourage healthy living and fitness among young people. I want children to be physically strong and mentally tensile. They will need to be because the future is going to get harder and more complex for the majority, if not all of them. Exercise and getting outside in the fresh air aren't just good for the heart and lungs but for the soul too. Sweat, toil and keeping active, are great educators! As Henry Ford once said, "Idleness is the reason for many of our troubles."[12].

I have tried to apply this same work ethic and principle throughout my life: endeavouring to achieve success at whatever it is I am tasked with. This has been especially true with personal fitness in my younger years, as previously shared. However, I was engaged in many worthwhile activities outside of the home, and this was not just limited to schooling, jogging long distances and weight training. These, and numerous other pursuits kept me busy - very busy! I had tenacity and inner drive, and my interests and commitments kept me sane and occupied. Simultaneously, I still fulfilled my house chores conscientiously, which included cleaning our younger sister's poo filled potty when she was a toddler – yes, that was a task we dreaded doing; plus washing up; setting and clearing the table. My bedroom was always kept meticulously tidy too, as was my personal appearance.

I wrote a poem in 2020, titled, My Teenage Years! It suitably depicts how busy and physically active I was in my youth.

My Teenage Years!

"Living on the Essex/East London border
Life at home created disorder
Siblings and I had it tough
Our best efforts never good enough.

Yet there were shining lights
Who illuminated a path bright
Salt of the earth friends
When life seemed a dead end.

Lesson 7 - Teamwork - We Are The Champions

High school was such a show
Woolly trousers made me scratch down below
Those cute girls had my attention
Struggled with algebra and had a few detentions.

Camping weekends with Dad
Drawing and art on my sketch pad
Wanted to be a Royal Marine
With my bowie knife trying not to be seen.

Hiding sprouts in my pocket
Cos if we didn't eat we'd get a rocket
Left over dinner on the table it would stay
Staring at us cold for breakfast the very next day.

Mine and Dad's trips to Smithfield
Picking up a turkey which had been killed
Chasing us through the doors
With its bloodied head and very sharp claws.

Lunch at school was no treat
Very little at home to really eat
The usual flattened cheese sarnie I'd make
Eventual free school meals were a welcome break.

Early morning Seminary at a crazy half past five
Followed by a morning paper round to strive
Jimmy Atkinson and I thus falling asleep
Each Sunday at the sacrament table in a heap.

At 14 Phil Dixon collecting me
Home Teaching in his disabled car with wheels just three
Sat tightly squeezed on the vehicle floor
Between his wheelchair and passenger door.

But pushing his wheelchair
Gave me a sense of care
My chocolate shirt and silver tie
Made me look like a mafia guy.

The Wright family were a huge blessing
Fourteen doors away was their setting
Paul West was a strength
Reaching out to me at any length.

Sneaking up to Tony White's brother's attic
Discovering the sound of Beach Boys so ecstatic
Bopping to Eddie Cochran was my chance
At the monthly Hyde Park youth dance.

At 15 near burst appendix a terrible ache
Refusing to drive me for goodness sake
Forced to walk to the doctors' a considerable way
Emergency op performed that very same day.

Intro to weights at fifteen
Looking like Arnie seemed a dream
Concrete floors and water from a tap
Nick Chapman and I committed during any cold snap.

Church Sports Day was an annual event
Hyde Park friends would frequent
6'4" Jimmy and I in the 5000 metres race
Overtaking me on the final bend at pace.

First ever date at eighteen
Cheryl Witham looked like a beauty queen
A walk to the cinema in a rain shower
My tiny brolly no room for me to cower.

At 18, during work lunch hour
For a friend, deceased records to scour
Recording names written down
At Somerset House, London Town.

Then in '84 I saw Gill on stage
Amazing voice at only 14 years of age
Years later, she would become my bride
And I'd have the most beautiful and adventurous ride.

So many were good to me
They allowed me to express and be free
Gratefully many are back in my life
May they all be blessed to prosper and thrive."

- By Grant J. Kersey

5th October 2020

Me at 18 years of age in the summer of '84.

Continuing the theme of physical fitness and the importance of having an inner drive, I recall a particularly satisfying memory when training to be a police officer at Hendon Police School. The recruits would be required to undertake a vast number of various learning skills, such as drill, parade inspections, law, police procedures, first aid, charitable work, unarmed self-defence, football tournaments, PE, swimming lessons, and monthly written exams. We also had the option of training for a certificate in lifesaving. Once again, as I like to aim high in whatever I put my mind to, I set my sights on the Gold Lifesaving Award. Why settle for second best when you are confident in your abilities to achieve the best?

Each week, we would have an hour or so training in the pool, in preparation for the test, which would be in the final week of our training – week 20. In order to be awarded the gold certificate, a recruit would need to successfully accomplish all ten tasks within the time allocated for each event. Some tasks were more strenuous than others, such as pulling an adult by their chin along the entire length, then pulling them by their chest for another length. Treading water with legs only, and arms raised high out of the water for about a minute, was also very difficult. By the end of the ninth event, I was very tired.

I had completed all nine events successfully, but in order to achieve gold, I now had to complete the final task, which required swimming three lengths in under two minutes. Determined as ever, I set off as fast as my arms could go. Halfway up the second length, I paused and held on to the side of the pool. One of the instructors lent down and said, "Well done lad! You did your best." He then reached out his arm to pull me out. I stretched out my arm, but immediately had a change of mind. No, I can do this!

I was in the 'zone' and burst into full speed. Out of the cor-

Lesson 7 - Teamwork - We Are The Champions

ner of my eye, at each breath, I could see my colleagues walking along, cheering me on. As I reached the end of the second length, I noticed that the digital clock positioned on the wall, was nearing 35 seconds. Without any further delay, I raced that final length like my life depended on it.

Touching the end of that third and final length, a roar of cheering, whistling and clapping erupted. I looked up at the digital clock - the seconds ticked down - 2,1,0. I had made it! My fellow recruits had championed and roared me on to success.

Unfortunately, I was too physically exhausted to get out of the pool by my own means, so my colleagues lifted me out and helped me to a corner. There I sat on the floor, breathing in oxygen from an oxygen tank and mask. I was completely shattered! I had pushed myself to the limit. I had done my very best!

Trying one's best in anything, which I encourage in schools, isn't necessarily all about the physical aspect. Often, it is about one's mentality, and in PE, I want children to believe in themselves and just do their best – though not to the extent where they need extra oxygen like I did that day!

Lesson 7 - Teamwork - We Are The Champions

My Gold Life Saving Certificate

Not surprisingly, if there is one lesson where a child is going to lose a shoe or an item of clothing, it is going to be when they are either getting changed for PE or changing back into their uniform. Goodness me, the number of times this has happened, especially with the little ones, is unbelievable. Missing socks, underwear, tights, vests, trousers and skirts. Putting another child's shoes on, or clothes inside out. The answer to most of these predicaments is simple: allow children to come to school already wearing their PE kit. Hey presto! No more Sherlock Holmes trying to solve the case of the missing sock! Plus, there'd be more time for the actual PE lesson. When the weather is cooler, they can wear tracksuit bottoms and a warm hoodie with the school badge on. I have observed several schools introducing this practical solution, but not nearly enough schools. However, coming to school wearing the school PE kit is not a rock-solid guarantee that items will still not disappear. I recall a PE lesson when one boy kicked a football so hard that one of his trainers shot through the air, like a swift bullet, and ended up on the school roof. He thought it was hilarious, as he hopped around with one trainer missing!

Furthermore, PE is the likeliest of lessons where a child will receive an injury. I've taught PE lessons that have ended in bumps, bruises, cuts and even a girl receiving an unfortunate broken nose because of another boy's recklessness with not adhering to the rules. Often it is that injured child, or another child, who has not followed my clear instructions and decided to do their own thing or were just plain careless. I have seen it happen several times, so now I give stricter instructions, and have seen the incidence of injuries decrease over recent years.

Depending upon the age group, I invite the children to have a little stretch to get those muscles warmed up. Then we have some warm-up exercises, including star jumps, jogging on the spot, and even press ups for the older children. No one was surprised when I introduced these exercises, together with some other PE routines, to my Year Five class at a school in mid-Dorset. Some of the children moaned at first, but they soon adapted to my lessons, and became more familiar with my warm-up routines. They also benefited from increased energy too. I was pleased to observe that the children who could barely manage one lap around the field when I started teaching them, were happily running several laps by the end of my two-term tenure.

Then in the summer, the school held its sports day. In front of parents and the entire school, all excitedly anticipating the forthcoming events, I proudly led my class onto the field and over to a shaded area. After placing their water bottles in a large tub, I asked the children to find a space, and, knowing the routine perfectly, they followed my instructions to the letter. We performed an eye-catching warm-up routine in front of the whole school, as well as parents and members of the local community. One of the points judges, named Julie, told me later how impressed both she and the headteacher had been. While we had been doing our warm-up, she had nudged the headteacher, Mr Carson, and said to him, "Look at that!" My class were the bee's knees! They were superb! They were like an efficient and organised unit, as each child kept in almost perfect timing. This was teamwork at it's very best!

In addition, I also love to take part in character or themed school dress up days too. Again, this is further evidence of teamwork and getting involved. Who doesn't like to dress up at school? Actually, I have encountered a few educators who hate it! Personally, I always enjoy the moment, and the children love it when their teachers show a sense of fun by joining in. Any educator, even a supply teacher, will be flavour of the month with the children when they do participate and dress up.

Here are a selection of photographs of me from several dress-up days, at different schools, over the years. Introducing the many faces of Mr Kersey:

Lesson 7 - Teamwork - We Are The Champions

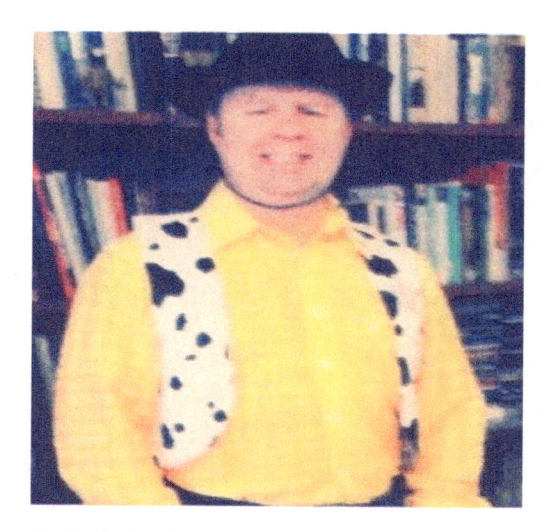

As Woody from 'Toy Story' for World Book Day in 2014.

As a Macbeth witch for Year Five Tudor topic in 2014.

Lesson 7 - Teamwork - We Are The Champions

As the bard, William Shakespeare, for Year Five Tudor topic in 2014.

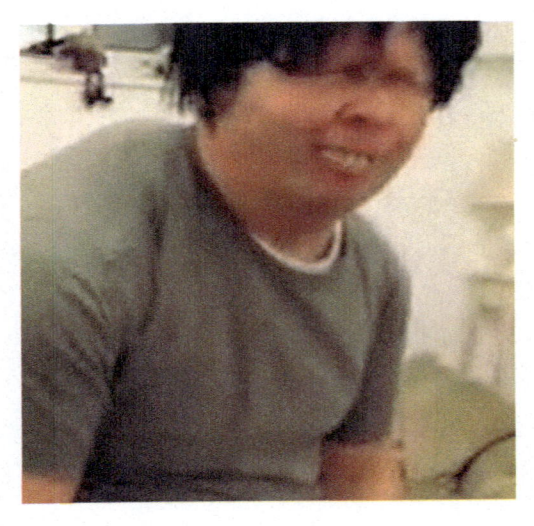

As the Hunchback of Notre Dame for World Book Day in 2015.

Lesson 7 - Teamwork - We Are The Champions

As Mr Twit from Roald Dahl's, The Twits, for World Book Day in 2017.

As 1980's 'athletes' for whole school Sport Relief Day in 2018.

Lesson 7 - Teamwork - We Are The Champions

As an 'imperial' Aztec chief for World Cup activities (class assigned Mexico) in 2018.

In 1940s dress for Year Five World War Two Topic School Trip in 2018.

Lesson 7 - Teamwork - We Are The Champions

World War Two Dress Up Day with two wonderful TAs: Trisha (left) and Sarah, in 2017.

Educators, but particularly leadership and teachers, are always in the spotlight, whether we like it or not. It comes with the job! However, there have been moments when I have shied away from the attention, often because the children have accomplished something astounding and deserve to be praised, rather than for accolades to be heaped on me. I'll share an example of this.

In spring 2014, I was teaching a Year Five class at a school in Bournemouth, when it was announced that the children were invited to participate in a nationwide writing competition. I believe this first stage of the competition was county-wide. After the rules and guidelines had been explained, we discussed our thoughts and ideas as a class, and then set about preparing for this exciting task. We decided as a year group to prepare the children carefully over a few days, rather than rushing headlong into it.

Entrants had to write a creative piece of writing, and most of the children in class seemed keen and interested. During our English sessions, we studied the features and techniques of successful creative writing, and I read stories and poetry to the class in character. I wanted each child to feel encapsulated, like they were there in the story or poem, and engaged both with me, and with each scenario being depicted, so that they would be more enthused about writing themselves. I enjoy reading to children, especially if there is the opportunity for me to get into character. One of my favourite books is Roald Dahl's, *The Twits*, and my favourite chapter from that book is Wormy Spaghetti. It is perfect to get into role because of the dialogue, plot and setting. I absorb myself as both Mr Twit and Mrs Twit. Using voices, facial expressions, body language, even a few extras not included in the book, such as a mouth burp while Mr Twit is scoffing his 'wormy' meal, I become the characters. The children absolutely love it and are totally absorbed.

So, I knew that if they were engaged and emotive, it would be communicated through their writing. They practised, edited and improved their written pieces until each child was able to produce work to a good or very high standard, which was then submitted for judging. We were all very excited as we anticipated any news!

Several weeks later, we received the news that one of the girls in my class, Janey, had achieved first place in her age group of 9-10 years. We were thrilled! Her parents were notified and invited to attend the awards ceremony at a local library. To my surprise, the headteacher, Mr Osgood, asked if I would also like to attend the event. I was grateful but felt a little uneasy. After all, I hadn't written the winning piece! I acknowledged Mr Osgood's appreciation but felt my attendance might detract from the kudos due to Janey. He reassured me and courteously replied, "You were part of the success Grant. You taught Janey what she needed to do to win. We'd love you to be at the ceremony, and I'm sure Janey's parents would like to see you there too. Please come along and join us!"

The award ceremony was held one afternoon during the Easter break, with dignitaries in attendance. The awards were presented to the winners of each category by the mayor and our member of parliament. Headteachers, teachers and winners with their parents, were gathered from across the county. It was a fabulous celebration, recognising the talents of many young people. I felt honoured to attend.

While the attention, quite rightly, was focused on Janey, I needed to accept that Mr Osgood wanted to thank me for my contribution by inviting me to attend the event. There is nothing wrong with receiving a little praise, direction, even correction from time to time. I have learned to be teachable over the years, and to accept help when it is offered. Success at school is a team effort, and together, we are all champions!

Epilogue

Well, there you have it! A snapshot of my seven years as a supply teacher on the south coast of England, and several relevant stories from my employment in the Metropolitan Police Service, and from my childhood.

I am conscious that my years in education will leave their mark on the impressionable young people I teach, as well as on some of the adults I encounter. When people are met with love, kindness and respect as they engage with others, it makes a difference. People, and that includes children, have equal moral worth, and good teachers recognise this. It is what many educators up and down the country and across the globe do every day. Everyone remembers that teacher, perhaps even that supply teacher, who made a difference, and they will be able to name them for years to come. I hope countless children will remember me as that nice teacher, who made them feel super special, and that none will think of me as being in any way, a nasty teacher. How we, as educators, treat the younger generation, will permeate their minds and help mould their futures. Their positive influence can echo through the decades.

Epilogue

Kudos to all educators but especially teachers. They go out of their way to give of themselves and their time, working long hours into the evenings and some of their weekend - but who gives time for them? Many are crying out for more support from leadership, Ofsted and the government, but very few are hearing them. In some cases, their concerns fall on deaf ears. They are struggling in large numbers, and innumerable teachers are wishing they could just leave the profession they once loved. Many others have already made that jump and taken early retirement or just quit the job and moved on to new horizons, where they can earn more money and perhaps feel more appreciated as well.

Until you have worked in a school or have a partner or relative who works as a teacher, you really don't know the full extent of workload they carry, day and night. Being a teacher can frequently feel like you have just run a marathon in the Sahara Desert with a heavy load on your back. Then as you crawl over the finish line, someone from leadership or a parent, decides to 'kick you in the face' telling you that you should have run faster. The 'dripping tap' must stop, or at least slow right down, otherwise that 'bucket' taking it all in, will just overflow. The mental health of educators must come first!

Teachers are amazing human beings! Who else, other than the parents or carers themselves, worries more about a child? Their everyday thinking is regularly absorbed in trying to resolve a problem, conflict, or learning dilemma, relating to one or more children

- even at the weekend. Teachers hold so many children into their hearts. They take on a whole lot too, and, in my opinion, do not receive the public recognition and credit they so deserve.

It takes maintaining your composure, when you are trying to calm a class of thirty unsettled children into their early morning work, while parents wish to privately speak to you at the same time.

It takes commitment when successive Governments continuously move the curriculum goalposts.

It takes creativity when you wish to teach a specific art lesson for that afternoon, only to discover at lunchtime, that the school has run out of the art supplies you desperately need.

It takes mindfulness when a child is struggling with a maths concept, and you want to encourage that child, without destroying their self-esteem.

It takes patience when you hear a child has distorted their account of an event you were involved in, and the parents want to speak to you, yet again, without notice.

It takes perseverance to cope with continuous on-going assessments and data collection.

It takes imagination to frequently update the displays on the four walls of your classroom, with bright, decorative and imaginative displays of learning and work, when you have no teaching assistant to help you.

It takes time management skills to somehow fit extra-curricular activities into your weekly timetable, following short notice.

It takes compassion and empathy when a child tells you their

Epilogue

pet dog died at the weekend, and they are struggling to focus on the day's learning.

It takes careful, detailed and flexible planning, when you have a class of thirty young minds all at different levels.

It takes professionalism when the school assigns a trainee teacher for you to train and mentor, and you know full well that that responsibility will drastically increase your workload overnight.

All the above, and much, much more, are expected of full-time, part-time and depending upon the type of assignment, supply teachers, HLTAs and TAs too. All educators are a credit to our society!

To this day, when I visit schools, the staff car park is often already full, despite the fact that I always aim for an 8a.m. arrival. I enter the classroom, knowing that, on the whole, I don't have to worry about preparing lesson plans, organising resources, completing assessments, data input, typing reports, running a club, attending staff meetings, planning meetings, parent meetings, year meetings, SEN meetings, pupil progress meetings, performance management meetings, any meetings, useless meetings, 'just for the sake of it' meetings!

I fulfil my role with total commitment, including tidying the classroom, completing all the marking and providing concise verbal or written feedback. I do this to make the teacher's job just that little bit easier. Only then do I go home. As I do so, I see the line of teachers' cars still there. Rarely, does a teacher leave school early.

Epilogue

They often take work home for the evening and at the weekend. Despite having once worked as a full-time teacher, after all these years as a supply teacher, I am even more aware and appreciative of the responsibilities of full-time and part-time teachers. I am humbled by the relatively easy task I have compared with theirs.

As for my failings, well, when I have failed, I have tried to do so with dignity and have learnt to move on from my mistakes. I still have the odd bad day at school. We all have the odd bad day at work, whatever our job or the setting. That's life! Tomorrow is always a new start. New days aren't just for the children but for us adults too. A profound quote I came across, fits perfectly with this mindset. "There is a reason the windshield is bigger than the rear-view mirror. Your future matters more than your past."[13]

On reflection, I am happy to continue working as a supply teacher. I have my evenings and weekends back, and I never have that 'sick feeling' on Sunday evenings, worrying that there is a myriad of work emails or text messages to write or respond to before going to work on Monday. I can attend social events over the weekend with no uneasy feeling that I should instead be at home writing reports, assessments, planning material for the following week, or marking all those books, which might be still sitting in the boot of my car.

Above all, I am now truly able to put my family first. I not only have the extra time to spend with my wife and children, but

I have the energy to do so. Supply teaching works for me and my family. Compared to when I was working as a full-time teacher, I am calmer. I am happier. I am healthier. I have time for myself again – and that, above all else, in this demanding and hectic world, is the most important thing.

References

1. Harding, Dr K. (2019) The Rabbit Effect – Live Longer, Happier, and Healthier with the Groundbreaking Science of Kindness. Available at: https://www.kellihardingmd.com/the-rabbit-effect (Accessed 4th June 2022).

2. Ginott, H.G. (1972) Teacher and Child. Available at: https://en.wikipedia.org/wiki/Haim_Ginott#Quotes_from_Teacher_and_Child (Accessed 4th June 2022).

3. Skavnak, B. (2018) Available at: https://www.bethenicekid.com (Accessed 4th June 2022).

4. Hepburn, A. (1993) Audrey Hepburn: An Intimate Portrait. Available at: https://libquotes.com/audrey-hepburn/quote/lbf1k2r (Accessed 4th June 2022).

5. Chaplin, C. Available at: https://www.thoughtco.com/ungorgettable-charlie-chaplin-quotes-2832435 (Accessed 4th June 2022).

6. Maroutian E. The Minds Journal. Available at: https://themindsjournal.com/anyone-who-makes-you-laugh-is-contributing-to-your-wellbeing/ (Accessed 4th June 2022).

7. Covey, S.R. (1989) The 7 Habits of Highly Effective People: Powerful Lessons in Personal Change. Available at: https://www.goodreads.com (Accessed 6th January 2019).

8. Gandhi, M. in Oliver Balch, "The relevance of Gandhi in the capitalism debate." Guardian (28th January 2013). Available at: https://www.theguardian.com/sustainable-business/blog/relevance-gandhi-capitalism-debate-rajni-bakshi (Accessed 4th June 2022).

9. MacDonald, G. (1877) The Marquis of Lossie. Available at: https://quotepark.com/quotes/1215125-george-macdonald-to-be-trusted-is-a-greater-compliment-than-to-be-l/ (Accessed 4th June 2022).

10. Williamson, G. in Sally Roach, "Ofsted Gets Thousands of Emails Praising Schools After Minister's Remarks." Guardian (12th January 2021). Available at: https://www.theguardian.com/world/2021/jan/12/ofsted-gets-thousands-of-emails-praising-schools-after-ministers-remarks (Accessed 4th June 2022).

11. Hardy, T. (2020) koimoi.com. Available at: https://www.koimoi.com/hollywood-news/tom-hardy-treating-janitor-with-same-respect-as-the-ceo-is-the-best-mondaymotivation-we-can-get/ (Accessed 4th June 2022).

12. Ford, H. (1944) Detroit Times. Available at: https://www.thehenryford.org/collections-and-research/digital-resources/popular-topics/henry-ford-quotes/ (Accessed 4th June 2022).

13. Lucado, M. (2017) Anxious for Nothing. Available at: https://www.quotenova.net/authors/max-lucado/qz79z3 (Accessed 4th June 2022).

Acknowledgements

The journey to finally completing and publishing this book has taken over four years; much longer than I had originally anticipated. I suppose that is because life doesn't stop when you begin writing a book. Along that road and by my side has been my wife. Thank you for your love and support Gill.

Thank you also to one of my former line managers, whose suggestion that I write a book about my stories and experiences in schools, lead me to this new and rewarding pathway.

Finally, I wish to thank several other friends who have helped me, in some way or another, with writing this book: graphic designer Russell Babidge and his wife, Elaine Babidge; the authors, Ros Lawrance and Claire 'Fairy' Colston; and finally, Lindsay Carruthers.

Song Title Acknowledgements

What a Wonderful World written by Bob Thiele and George David Weiss.
Make 'Em Laugh written by Arthur Freed and Nacio Herb Brown.
What's Going On written by Marvin Gaye, Renaldo Benson and Al Cleveland.
Help! Written by John Lennon and Paul McCartney.
Don't Stop Believin' written by Steve Perry, Jonathan Cain and Neal Schon.
Don't Worry, Be Happy written by Bobby McFerrin.
We Are The Champions written by Freddie Mercury.
Rockabilly Rebel written by Steve Bloomfield.
YMCA written by Jacques Morali and Victor Willis.
We Will Rock You written by Brian May.
Right Here, Right Now written by Mike Edwards.

Picture Permissions
All photographs are from the author's personal collection.

Text Permissions
The author gratefully acknowledges permission to print text and images relating to the following individuals and book:
Dr Kelli Harding, MD, MPH – The Rabbit Effect: Live Longer, Happier, and Healthier with the Groundbreaking Science of Kindness.
Nadene Lomu, wife of former New Zealand rugby player and legend, Jonah Lomu.

About the Author

Grant was born in the East End of London and raised on the Essex/East London border. He was the oldest of six children, who came from various parentage, including the youngest, who was a foster child with Downs Syndrome. Extreme adversity in his childhood taught him resilience and tenacity, and to appreciate the values of hope, love and kindness.

After leaving school, he worked as an administrative clerk for a prominent solicitor firm in London, before embarking on a voluntary service assignment in the USA. That experience consolidated his love for America and its warm-hearted people. Two years later, he returned to the UK, and worked as a labourer, taper and jointer, then roofer, before finally joining the Metropolitan Police Service.

Eleven years after joining the Met, he and his young family emigrated to Australia. It was an experience he will always be grateful for. The Australian people, in his opinion, were some of the most down-to-earth people he had ever met. Five years later, the entire family returned to Old Blighty, where he enrolled at university, and ultimately gained a 2:1 degree in Primary Education.

Ten years residing on England's south coast and very close to the beaches, while working as a teacher, and then a supply teacher, gave his family a fun and healthy lifestyle. Now, mainly for economic reasons, they live elsewhere in the UK. It remains to be seen where their next adventure takes them.

Printed in Great Britain
by Amazon